Only the Good Invest Young

A New Financial Leader Starts the Fire

William Kelly

Kelly Financial Services, LLC
Braintree, Massachusetts

William Kelly/Kelly Financial Services LLC
10 Forbes Road, Suite 130
Braintree, MA 02184
www. kellyfinancial.org

Book Layout ©2025 Advisors Excel, LLC

Ordering Information:
Quantity sales. Special discounts are available on quantity purchases by corporations, associations, and others. For details, contact the "Special Sales Department" at the address above.

Only the Good Invest Young / William Kelly. —1st ed.
ISBN 979-8-9937624-0-1

Contents

Dedicated to my father, Bill Kelly (1952 - 2017)

I love you beyond words. I miss you beyond anything tangible.

And for those who need guidance,

This is for you!

"Never quit."

—Dad

Introduction

Why should I read this book?

I believe many young investors are out there but haven't yet unlocked their full potential. Many people have the fire and desire to make their money work for them. Thanks to the interconnectedness of today's global economy, we have a unique ability to put the money we've earned into systems that can help it grow. With the proper guidance, knowledge, and trust in these systems, we can turn hard work into lasting wealth. In my opinion, this isn't just a relationship — it's an extraordinary **opportunity**.

To answer the question directly, I would say:

I believe you can build a better future.

Even at a young age, I've already met numerous people my age who feel stuck, unsure of how to navigate the world of investing or build a solid financial future. It became clear to me that it's not just retirees who need guidance and structure — young people like us do, too.

I consider myself an old soul. While I sometimes feel disconnected from my Gen Z peers, I still share many formative experiences — we grew up playing the same video games, watching the same TV shows and YouTube videos, and living through the same defining moments. What sets me apart is the perspective I gained from my baby boomer parents. Their respect for tradition, disciplined financial habits, and long-term planning shaped my understanding of building a secure future.

Our generation could profoundly benefit from this kind of mindset. Observing my peers, I've realized the value of an outsider's perspective, especially one grounded in knowledge and experience. I've learned from various mentors, including my parents, sister, members of our family business, entrepreneurs, and talented investors. These lessons give me deep insight from which to draw.

However, this book isn't about me or my upbringing; it's about addressing a problem I've observed. I've met brilliant young people, including child prodigies, at one of the top prep schools in the country. However, the question, "What's your plan for the future?" —be it regarding investing, retirement, or asset management — often left people without a clear response. This book is my way of guiding them — and anyone eager to learn — to map out a clear and confident path toward their future.

Through these interactions, I understand the significance of my role as an investment writer in today's world. To every young person reading right now:

Only the Good Invest Young!

And please, let me help you!

Clear any doubts or hesitation from your mind. Throughout this book, I'll address questions and share insights on planning for the rest of your life. This book is for those who aim to achieve financial success in the investment world later in life, while building good financial habits and lasting wealth. I am not a day-trader. If you're seeking day-trading tips, stop reading now and toss this book out the window — or better yet, pass it on to someone ready to take a long-term approach.

I've written this to offer you sound guidance for managing your money, with the hope and goal that you'll have even more of it by the time you've completed your career. This endeavor is about giving you the chance for a beautiful future and retirement (or later adult life) because you made smart decisions today. The result? More time with your family, freedom from worrying about debt or bills, and extra wealth for you and your loved ones to enjoy.

I was born into this discipline. As a child, my father often brought me to work with him, immersing me in this world from an early age. Over time, as I became more involved, my roles shifted toward service and education. I've had the privilege and honor of growing up surrounded by this field and some of its greatest professionals. I've spent countless hours sitting in on client meetings, gaining insight, and understanding that few have the chance to experience so young.

I believe our family business has attracted some of the industry's most talented and respected advisors. They've shared with me invaluable knowledge that you can learn too. Much of what I'll share stems from their foundational principles and unique wisdom. Long before I entered the investment industry, I spent years interacting with our remarkable clients. We support them with sound guidance, actively manage their plans, and, in many ways, they guide us, too. Please note that I am not a financial adviser, and this information is for general discussion or educational purposes only. It is not individualized investment or financial advice.

We take great pride in fostering a collaborative environment, working as a team to help ensure our clients are set up for success and positioned in a way that aligns with their goals and values.

While we're on the topic …

Now, it's time for us to start thinking seriously about our financial futures. If we want to outperform our parents and grandparents, we must start the process right and, most importantly, **early**! The people who need the most attention right now are **you**! By "you," I mean those aged eighteen to twenty-eight. But this still applies to you even if you're thirty or forty. You're still young in the eyes of the market, and this is the perfect time to start planting the right seeds.

That's enough of the introduction — dive in and enjoy the book! I hope it provides you with valuable insights and, above all, helps you achieve remarkable results.

If you'd like to reach out for any reason, email me at:

williamkellyjr@kellyfinancial.org

CHAPTER 1

What are the Chances?

I'll start this chapter with one of my all-time favorite market stories. This is the tale of Chance. I remember sharing it with our Senior Vice President Advisor after leaving a restaurant in Seaport. I first came across it in the book *Common Sense on Mutual Funds* by Vanguard's legendary and late founder, John C. Bogle. It's an excellent read — I highly suggest it. Bogle references the character Chance the Gardener (also known as Chauncey Gardiner) from Jerzy Kosinski's novel *Being There*.

The story begins with Chance, an intellectually handicapped gardener who spends his entire life working on a secluded estate. His world is confined within the walls of a mansion, shielding him from the outside and exposing him only to the garden he diligently tends. With no formal education or external influences, Chance sees things exactly as they appear, free from complication or pretense.

The elderly and highly successful businessman who owns this mansion eventually passes away, and the property is sold. A new wealthy businessman takes possession, and while Chance continues as the estate's gardener, there is one key difference. Unlike the previous owner, this new businessman actually speaks with Chance. Their conversations sometimes veer into business matters, with the owner asking for Chance's thoughts on challenges in the investment firm he runs. Chance, who knows only gardening, offers blunt, unfiltered responses often rooted in analogies to nature. To the businessman, these seem like profound insights. To Chance, they are simply honest observations.

One day, the businessman, impressed by Chance's simplicity and clarity, offers him an advisory role at the company board meetings. These sessions are critical to the firm's success, and Chance, unknowingly elevated to the role of a modern-day prophet, joins them as a voice of reason.

On his first day in this new capacity, the board convenes during a severe market crash. The tension in the room is palpable. Executives are panicked, sweating, and visibly distressed about the future of their business. But Chance remains calm, unshaken by their worries. He stands up, walks to the head of the table, looks around the room, and says plainly, "Everything will be fine."

The atmosphere shifts. Some laugh nervously, others look incredulous, but everyone listens. Chance then explains:

"Well, your market works a lot like my garden. Each company has its roots. Each business starts as a seed, and the more nurturing it receives, the more it grows. It thrives longer, and with proper care and consistent nurturing, it can reach its full potential, increasing its chances of survival. Once the roots are firmly in place, it's quite set, really."

One board member challenges him, "That's great and all, but everything in the foreseeable market is collapsing, and our business is dependent on the market. A collapse is imminent!"

Chance replies, his expression unchanged, "Yes, it does look that way. You must understand what I mean, though. When my plants finally sprout and grow, they eventually produce a leaf, a flower, or a berry. It yields something beautiful and good. The plant may live for a long time, but it does not stay that way forever, does it?"

The businessmen sit there listening intently.

Chance continues, "When winter or fall comes, so does what looks like death and destruction for my plants. Those things are not true. The roots are still intact. The harsh conditions force them to hibernate. As long as your businesses are in the market, and the market is in its nation, and the nation still has its earth, the roots will not cease to exist ... You know, sometimes I have to deadhead some of the plants in the garden, but every time I do, the plant's beauty comes back to me in time. Sometimes the winter will be harsh. I know the plants and trees save all of the life they can and hold still. Once winter passes, they'll return back to me. Every now and then, a storm will seemingly wipe my garden away, but I knew the plants that had left their roots were going to be the ones coming back."

The executives sit silently, captivated by the wisdom in his words. What Chance has said isn't some intricate financial analysis or high-stakes strategy. It is, simply, the truth. A truth that resonates at the core of their fears.

Taking Chance's advice to heart, the board convinces their clients to hold firm in their investments. While competitors panic and sell off, their firm stands resilient. When the market rebounds, they not only survive but thrive, outperforming competitors who had succumbed to fear, all thanks to the gardener who saw the world through the lens of his flowers and roots.

What can we take from Chance's story?

Chance teaches us an important lesson about the truth behind "seeing isn't believing." Just because your account balance is down or the market is in a recession doesn't mean it's the end. It isn't over if you still hold that stock or mutual fund. It may be simply a rough season or storm that you need to weather. However, with that being said, the risk of an investment completely going to zero is still real and should be considered.

The key is to stay strong and diligent with your investments. If every investor panicked and thought like the competition in Chance's story, much of the structure of today's market wouldn't exist. This reaction is precisely why I stand by the principles of long-term investing combined with detailed, forward-looking planning. It's the most consistent way to grow wealth for the future while minimizing risk — apart from having a steady job, of course.

If you think of a better way, call me.

Second, it's easy to become clouded when overstimulated by the constant motion around us, the responsibilities we shoulder, and the goals we chase. Chance didn't have those distractions, which kept him from being clouded. He was headstrong yet honest, two incredibly valuable qualities. Now, I'm not suggesting you abandon everything essential and live a simple life. That would be impractical advice unless you plan to become a Shaolin monk.

It's possible to apply Chance's philosophy to your life and decision-making without giving up your jobs, goals, dreams, assets, or future plans. Finance legend and former Fidelity Magellan fund manager Peter Lynch said it best in his 1989 classic *One Up on Wall Street*: The most crucial qualities for successful investing are "patience, self-reliance, common sense, a tolerance for pain, open-mindedness, detachment, persistence, humility, flexibility, a willingness to do independent research (like you're doing reading this book), an equal willingness to make mistakes, and the ability to ignore general panic." I couldn't agree more with that philosophy.

To make sound investment decisions, you need the knowledge to evaluate if your investments are stable and tied to strong companies, even during temporary downturns, and the discipline to stay vigilant. Reflect on whether the company has solid foundations and a history of bouncing back. If the answer is "yes," it's often wise to remain invested and consider adding more to your position. On the other hand, if you conclude "no" for any reason, it might be better to sell and reallocate your funds to stronger opportunities.

I hate to see anyone leave their money tied up in a low-quality company. That said, life doesn't always go as planned, and losses or sunk costs are inevitable. And that's okay. I'd be more worried if you went through your investing life without learning from a loss.

A sunk cost is a loss you can't recover. When it happens, you pick yourself up and keep moving forward toward your goals. You don't stop. Strength and fortitude are essential traits for successful, long-term investing. It might sound odd, but trust me, if you stay strong and disciplined, you're less likely to falter and far more likely to grow. Discipline is crucial in this area of life. It allows you to rise above emotional stock trading and make better decisions.

I believe one of the most important thing to focus on is a company's ethics, mission, and goals. While it's impossible to methodically predict the future market, one thing you can rely on is a business's purpose, values, and motives. These ideals should remain constant. After all, how could you expect a company with shifting philosophies to maintain consistency in other areas?

If a company operates with strong values — like advancing innovation, fostering growth, or contributing to the betterment of the world — it seems like a reasonable investment choice. When you buy equity in a company, you're investing in its success and prosperity. I prefer supporting companies that push boundaries and drive progress to the next level. However, you may have different preferences, such as investing in long-term, stable companies. There's no one-size-fits-all approach, and how you choose to invest is entirely up to you.

If you want to gain the ability to own investments, especially as a young adult, there are two essential areas to address: budgeting and spending. Let's dive in and explore these basics together.

CHAPTER 2

Budgets, Buffers, and Big Flex Credit

Assets and Budgeting Basics

If there's one key foundation for everything finance-related, it's your savings and budget.

Our company's first step with clients is reviewing their assets and current budget. This strategy is essential. Without this information, we can't create a successful and well-thought-out plan for your future. If a client didn't provide complete details about their savings, reliable budget, or estate, I wouldn't feel confident designing any part of their financial strategy. The more information you share, the stronger and more effective the plan will be.

Fortunately, we have fantastic clients, so we don't encounter that issue, as understanding finances is a key part of working with a financial advisor. However, I've noticed that many people my age struggle to get a solid handle on their finances.

Let's map out your income, budget, and assets. Grab a pen and paper.

- **Do the math**: Calculate your annual earnings based on your work rate. Don't forget to account for time off, like PTO or sick days.

- **Outline your monthly (or chosen time frame) budget**: Include categories like food, entertainment, and subscriptions.
- **Take stock of your investments**: Do you own small-caps? Major stocks like NVDA, AAPL, MSFT, or AMZN? What about foreign securities, bonds, or other significant assets? Consider appreciating or depreciating items such as cars, watches, or jewelry.

Great work! You've started tracking three of the most important aspects of your finances. Honestly, track as much as you can. The more you track, the better. This will not only boost your confidence but also give you a deeper understanding and sense of control over your finances. You'll be able to see where you stand and where you might be heading.

If you're around my age, chances are you've recently finished high school or college and may still be living with your parents. That's fantastic! Living rent-free can save you a ton of money. But if you're like many young people with summer or weekend jobs, **do not** waste all that hard-earned money. You shouldn't spend every dollar you earn — save some after covering necessities like tuition, car insurance, food, and rent.

The money you save now has the potential to grow in the market over time, ideally for retirement or long-term goals (unless it's emergency savings). You can only plan your investments once you know exactly what you own and earn. And don't forget to stay on top of how you invest your money — I'll cover that more later.

If you don't have a firm grasp or control over your finances, how can you expect to grow or invest them successfully? Take the time to track, understand, and manage your money. It's the first step towards building a secure financial future.

It's just as important to take a close look at your expenses. We live in a system of give-and-take with the market — that's the nature of a free-market economy, and there's nothing wrong with that. The key is to help ensure you're navigating it wisely and strategically.

Now comes the fun part: the trackables. Costs and expenses. Let's break them down so you can gain a clearer understanding and take control of your financial picture.

- **Organize your Fixed Costs**: These are consistent expenses with little to no fluctuation in price or billing, typically covering essential needs. Simply put, they are costs that rarely change and are necessary — electricity, rent, or internet bills.

- **Variable Costs**: These are similar to fixed costs but tend to fluctuate more. Examples include gas and groceries. Changes in factors like administration, shortages, surpluses, or supply and demand can all influence the price of these items.

- **Unpredictable Expenses**: These include things like yearly memberships or holiday gifts. Their prices can vary widely, making them harder to predict. However, you can estimate an average for these expenses by tracking your spending regularly. This exercise allows you to gauge their cost on a quarterly, annual, or other long-term basis to better plan for them.

Emergency Fund

Life comes with its share of costs, especially variable and unpredictable ones. That's why it's crucial to have a fallback in the form of an untouched and steadily growing **emergency fund**. Life is full of surprises, and nobody can predict what expenses might pop up. Your car's bumper might fall off mid-drive. A hurricane could blow your fence away. Your phone might slip and disappear into the abyss of a sewer grate. Or you could face an emergency trip to the hospital.

During economic or market stress, having a safety net can be the difference between a manageable setback and a financial disaster. Your backup cash can keep things from spiraling out of control. To further illustrate the importance of an emergency fund, here are six key reasons, including some of what we've just touched on, but in greater detail.

Unexpected Expenses

Life can surprise us with unexpected costs, like medical emergencies, sudden car repairs, or urgent home maintenance problems. An emergency fund allows you to handle these expenses without resorting to debt, especially high-interest options like credit cards or payday loans.

Job Loss or Income Disruption

Job loss, furloughs, or significant income reductions can happen due to economic downturns, industry changes, or company restructuring. An emergency fund helps cover your living expenses during these times, giving you the financial breathing room to find new employment. It also spares you from selling off investments at a bad time, which could lock in losses or derail your long-term financial plans.

Avoiding Debt

Without an emergency fund, unexpected costs may push you to depend on credit cards or loans, often with high-interest rates. This situation can lead to mounting debt, creating an additional financial strain. If you find it hard to make timely payments, it can also take a toll on your credit score, impacting your financial health further.

Financial Independence

An emergency fund plays a vital role in achieving financial independence. It empowers you to make decisions that align with your long-term personal and professional goals, rather than letting immediate financial pressures force you into choices.

Peace

Having a financial cushion can significantly reduce the stress and anxiety of spending, making life less stressful and a bit more vibrant. The mental and emotional relief it provides is invaluable — truly. It enables you to tackle challenges head-on without the looming fear of financial ruin. That's a game changer, and arguably the most compelling reason to have an emergency fund.

Flexibility in Decision-Making

An emergency fund gives you the freedom to make choices that might otherwise be out of reach. For example, you could seize unexpected opportunities like enrolling in a career development course, starting a backyard project, or investing in an appreciating asset like gold or silver — all without the burden of financial stress.

Economic or Market Stress

In periods of economic downturn or market volatility, your investments could suffer temporary losses. An emergency fund provides a safety net, allowing you to avoid selling investments in a down market to raise cash. This approach prevents you from locking in losses and helps preserve your ability to benefit from future market recoveries.

If you consistently contribute to and preserve an emergency fund, you prepare yourself to **handle uncertainty.** Ideally, this fund should cover three to six months of living expenses. If that's not feasible, contribute as much as you realistically can without sacrificing your standard of living or dignity. Building and maintaining an emergency fund is a foundational aspect of sound financial planning — planning for emergencies is essential.

Debt and Credit Scores

Do not forget to manage your **debt**. Sure, having no debt is ideal, but a little isn't always bad. What truly matters is your credit score, which you start building as soon as you turn eighteen and step into adulthood. You have probably heard of people with "poor credit." These are often folks who are reluctant or fail to pay their bills on time. If you have a higher credit score, lenders and financial institutions will view you more favorably when you apply for loans or financial products. It reflects your accountability and ability to pay your bills on time and in full.

In many of life's transactions, a low credit score can be a significant barrier. For example, your credit score isn't just important for securing loans — it's also a key factor when renting an apartment or property. Landlords often check your credit, and in many cases, it will determine whether they'll offer you a lease. Even if you still secure a rental contract with a low credit score, you might face larger security deposits.

Even certain employers check credit scores. Your credit score can even impact your ability to get insurance or certain utility services. So, the best thing you can do is avoid taking on more than you can repay and always pay your bills on time. Truly focus on maintaining a good credit score throughout your adult life. Poor financial decisions with debt will only lead to additional stress and unnecessary suffering. But hey, if that's your goal, let's grab coffee — I've got questions!

We've covered the basics of budgeting, credit, and debt. My hope? That you will begin thinking bigger, broader, and stay consistent for *years*. My bet? Most of you have more potential than you realize. So, kick the bad habits and adopt the good ones. Here's a simple starting point: identify where you're wasting money on things you don't need, then invest that money instead. It's not rocket science, but it does take healthy discipline. Think of the payoff. Emergency savings, a retirement nest egg, a college fund for your future kids — it's about setting yourself up for the next chapter in life.

I will say that method comes with its imperfections. It's a classic example of the "save money, don't indulge" mindset, which can sometimes lead to unhappiness. People don't always need to pare down the simple pleasures they enjoy.

While making that choice can be helpful, the more money you earn, the more you should ideally allocate to investments. Once you earn a substantial income, something like a $5 coffee makes proportionally less of a difference if you invest it instead. As you'll read, it's generally advisable to devote 15 percent of your pretax pay to investing.[1]

As you get older and take on higher-paying jobs, whether climbing the corporate ladder, focusing on developing self-employment work, or expanding your business, your investments should grow proportionally to your income.

---

[1] Elizabeth Gravier. CNBC Select. July 30, 2023. "This is how much of your income should go toward investing, according to experts"
https://www.cnbc.com/select/how-much-of-your-income-should-go-toward-investing/

CHAPTER 3

Never Forget the Dutch

Thanks to the Dutch, we've achieved something marvelous in our free market nation and world.

Many of you who took a trade or economics class have heard the epic story of the birth of public investment. It began with the Dutch East India Company in 1602. The company created a public asset-selling system where they would receive funding in return for selling pieces of the company. This system provided equal opportunities for people of all wealth levels, without discrimination, as it didn't matter who specifically purchased the shares.[2]

This model laid the foundation for modern public companies that serve their shareholders by creating value and generating returns. While the role of public companies in serving broader societal interests is often debated, the principle of offering individuals a stake in a business remains a cornerstone of the global economy today.

So, next time you see a Dutch person, give them my regards!

If you've read this far, you most likely have gathered a lot of new knowledge about the market, or a refresher at a minimum. To many of

[2] Farhan Rafid. Euro News. June 4, 2025. "How a Dutch trading company started the World's First Stock Exchange"
https://www.euronews.com/business/2025/04/13/how-a-dutch-trading-company-started-the-worlds-first-stock-exchange

you, these are terms you're hearing for the first time. It's about time you have a better understanding of them.

Below are the four most common financial investments. An investor can hold these for either the long or short term. Each vehicle has benefits and drawbacks.

Stocks

According to the Merriam-Webster Dictionary:

Stock [stäk]

a: the proprietorship element in a corporation, usually divided into shares and represented by transferable certificates

b: a portion of such stock of one or more companies

Care to guess which culture coined the investment term "stock"? You got it! The term has its roots in the Dutch word **"stok"**, which means "stick" or "tree trunk." In the sixteenth and seventeenth centuries, during the rise of Dutch trade and finance, those growing sectors used the word metaphorically to represent a financial stake or capital in a venture.

Stocks are divided shares (usually a small percentage of a company) made available by a corporation to be bought by a consumer like you and me, to fund the issuing corporation. McDonald's, for example, "went public" with an initial public offering (IPO) in 1965.[3] The executives decided, "Let's take a portion of our company, divide it into tiny pieces, and allow people to buy and sell it to each other, so we receive the funding and make the capital we need." Essentially, they sell part of their company when they need money, and once it's "out there," the public actively trades it. It's a very unique and intricate system.

When you buy a corporation's "stock," to an extent, you indirectly buy into its wins and losses. Many external variables, such as the overall economy, politics, and investor perceptions, feed into the stock's price at any given time. However, part of a stock's price reflects the

---

3 McDonald's. 2025. "McDonald's Stock Information.
https://corporate.mcdonalds.com/corpmcd/investors/stock-information.html

corporation's internal operations, financial outcomes, and management strategies.

A company's intrinsic value influences its stock price, and vice versa. The intrinsic value of a stock is its *true worth* based on the company's fundamentals, such as earnings, assets, and future growth potential. It represents what the stock should be worth, regardless of its current market price, and investors often use it to identify undervalued or overvalued opportunities.

There's an old expression: "Buy low, sell high." When the stock price is high, it can be a great time to sell. Conversely, when the price decreases, it's often seen as a less favorable time to sell. However, a drop in stock price can present an excellent opportunity to buy or add to your existing investment — especially if the company is strong and well-established, like McDonald's. By purchasing more shares while the price is low, you position yourself to recover losses and potentially earn additional profits when the stock value rises again. It's a straightforward strategy.

Stock investing is **risky** because the price and value of stocks can fluctuate significantly due to factors like market volatility, economic conditions, company performance, and investor sentiment. You could lose part or all of your investment if the stock price drops, the company underperforms, or it goes bankrupt. Additionally, external factors like geopolitical events, interest rate changes, or unexpected news can impact stock prices unpredictably, making it challenging to guarantee returns.

These are the very basics of stock investing. Their risk and volatility open the door for opportunity. The analysis becomes more detailed and focused when it pertains to the different types of stocks. There are categories of stocks in the market, which help us discern and organize our investments based on the industries or traits associated with each category. While not an all-inclusive list, some of these categories are listed below.

To quickly mention, there are some terms I haven't covered yet. Two I want to explain are "aggressive" and "conservative" assets. Simply put, conservative investments are long-term (usually), low-risk assets. Aggressive investments are high-risk, high-reward/loss assets.

Blue-chip stocks are large, well-established companies, many of which are part of the S&P 500® index. The S&P 500® represents 500 of the largest publicly traded companies available on the market. These stocks typically belong to industry-leading giants known for their stability and reliability. However, being large and established doesn't mean they are completely risk-free. Still, don't let fear come into the equation of decision-making. These companies are generally considered solid options for long-term investing.

Growth stocks are shares in companies expected to grow at a faster rate than the overall market. These companies typically reinvest their earnings into their own development and expansion rather than focus on reaping immediate profits. Essentially, they grow rapidly, but don't focus on returns for the investor through dividends. Their value lies in their potential for long-term capital appreciation.

Emerging market stocks are a distinct category and should not be confused with growth stocks. Emerging stocks are shares of companies in developing countries. They typically focus on industries or businesses with significant potential in these emerging economies. While they offer promising opportunities, their defining feature is their origin in less developed markets. For U.S. investors, emerging market stocks can provide a chance to diversify portfolios and tap into the growth potential of developing economies, but they also come with higher risks due to economic and political instability in these regions.

Dividend stocks (common and preferred stock) are shares in public companies that pay you for owning their stock. Dissimilar to growth stocks, you receive payment (usually quarterly) from the firm that prioritizes returning a portion of its profits to its investors. While not a hard-and-fast rule, dividend stocks are generally less volatile than growth stocks. However, these stocks do not grow as rapidly in comparison. Common stockholders usually have voting rights, which preferred shareholders don't receive. Also, common stockholders are more likely to gain preemptive rights, which is essentially the priority for purchasing new shares issued.

Small-cap stocks, typically with market capitalizations between $300 million and $2 billion, represent smaller or mid-sized businesses that, while riskier due to their less-established nature, offer immense growth potential. However, don't let their volatility and lack of dividends fool you. I know many people who sold their investments in Apple (sadly) before it became a global giant. Remember, they were a small-cap company at one point, too, along with Google, Microsoft, Visa, and Netflix. While volatile, investing in small caps could pay off long term if you're patient and diversify wisely, as you never know which company could become the next major success story.

Bonds

Again, according to the Merriam-Webster Dictionary:

Bond [bänd]
a: an interest-bearing certificate of public or private indebtedness

Bonds, a type of debt security, are generally regarded as a safe, protective asset. They typically maintain stability and provide fixed, unchanging returns. For companies, governments, or other entities, issuing bonds can be a source of capital. These entities reach out to the public and say, "If you loan us money, we promise to return your money to you with interest after a while, so you'll end up earning more." The issuer backs some bonds with its word or trust (known as debentures), while others are backed by pledged assets (like real estate or government security).

When you buy a bond, you essentially act as a lender. You lend money and, in return, earn interest while also receiving your full initial investment back when the bond reaches maturity. Generally, bonds are considered safer than stocks, but unfortunately, there's a risk. If an issuing company is weak, increasingly declining, or defaulting, the company could collapse. However, as you provide money through a debt security, you are a **creditor.** The company would prioritize repaying you, the indebted, before anyone else, unless it goes completely bankrupt. However, that is the worst case scenario and is less common in reputable companies.

There are also rating scales available, from Standard & Poor, for example, that help you determine if a bond is rated AAA (utmost quality) or as low as D (practically in default). Following that note, the ones you may want to avoid, unless you wish to take on the risk, are the extremely high-interest or volatile company debt securities, known as **junk bonds**, because, as the term states, you're putting your money in volatile "junk." That's like taking your dad's old truck that has 300,000 miles and has been loafing in the external elements for years and putting a bunch of money into it. Literally anything could happen to it. The exhaust falls off, a piston shoots out, you name it. It's better to buy a more reliable car than to invest money you know is at high risk of being lost.

The difference between vehicles and bonds is that vehicles depreciate and don't accrue value, unless they're classics. Bonds are loans offered to increase your investment while providing capital to companies, governments, and other entities. Bonds are usually offered at par value (or face value). The par value is the base amount (not including interest) the company is required to pay you at maturity, as listed on the bond when you buy it. Like stocks, bonds fluctuate in value based on supply and demand, but the par-value does not change. For clarity, I've provided the following example.

Credit Ratings

	S&P	Moody's	Fitch	Kroll
Investment Grade	AAA	Aaa	AAA	AAA
	AA	Aa	AA	AA
	A	A	A	A
	BBB	Baa	BBB	BBB
Non-Investment Grade	BB	Ba	BB	BB
	B	Ba	B	B
	CCC	Caa	CCC	CCC
	CC	Ca	CC	CC
	C	C	C	C
	D	D	D	D

[4]

Bond A is listed at a par value of $1,000 (the typical par value for bonds) with an interest rate of 5 percent and a maturity of ten years.

---

[4] DebtBook. 2025. "What is the Role of the Rating Agency?"
https://www.debtbook.com/learn/blog/who-are-the-rating-agencies

However, the bond's price is only $900, because a massive surplus is lying around. Let's say you bought the bond at $900. The bond issuer owes you $1,000 (a $100 profit off the bat!) along with semi-annual payments of 2.5 percent (as bonds usually distribute their interest payments semi-annually) of the par ($25) for the next 10 years ($500). Isn't that cool? Not only are you profiting from the interest but buying the bond at a discount gives you an added profit at maturity.

Like all things, if there are discounts, premiums will serve as the inverse. In this separate example, imagine you study the bond market and see Bond B with the usual par of $1,000, featuring a great interest rate of 10 percent, and a maturity of ten years. It seems good so far, but then you notice the bond price is $1,100, a $100 premium over the par value! Yikes.

Assume both bonds are ten years out from maturity. The following chart breaks down the cash flows and net profit, assuming both bonds are ten years from maturity. It also presents a picture of the cumulative advantage of compound interest.

Aspect	Bond A	Bond B
Face Value	$1,000	$1,000
Purchase Price	$900 (discounted)	$1,100 (premium)
Interest Rate	5% (compounded semi-annually)	10% (compounded semi-annually)
Semi-Annual Interest Payment (1st Period)	$25 ($1,000 x 2.5%)	$50 ($1,000 x 5%)
Cash Flows:		
- Initial Payment	-$900	-$1,100
- Total Interest Earned Over 10 Years, Reinvested (Compounded Semi-Annually)	$645.31	$1,628.89
- Face Value Paid at Maturity	$1,000	$1,000
Total Cash Flow at Maturity	$1,645.31 ($1,000 + $645.31 interest)	$2,628.89 ($1,000 + $1,628.89 interest)
Net Profit/Loss	$745.31 ($1,645.31 - $900 initial cost)	$1,528.89 ($2,628.89 - $1,100 initial cost)

One last important thing to mention: certain types of bonds are treated and taxed differently. For example, corporate bonds (the ones any old business would issue) are taxed at the state and federal levels. Treasury bills (a.k.a. T-bills, with a maturity of one year or less), Treasury notes (a.k.a. T-notes, with a maturity of two to ten years), or Treasury bonds (a.k.a. T-bonds, with a maturity of twenty to thirty years) are exempt from state taxation but not exempt from federal taxes. Municipal (city, county, or school) bonds are completely tax exempt from federal and state taxes. These bonds often fund infrastructure.

You would probably consider only investing in the last four for tax efficiency — which is the incentive — but government bonds usually pay lower interest rates than corporate bonds. Nevertheless, just because a corporate bond might offer higher returns than a municipal bond doesn't mean it will make you more money after paying taxes. Sometimes, municipal bonds or Treasury offerings can earn you more due to their tax exemptions despite paying lower interest rates.

Separately, you may have heard people say they are on a "fixed income." For example, in the scene from *The Incredibles*, Mr. Incredible helps his client, Mrs. Hogenson. She pleads with him after having insurance claims denied, and says, "I'm on a fixed income!" Among other forms of fixed income — such as Social Security, pensions, and retirement account withdrawals it's likely that people who make this claim own bonds in some capacity. These are probably low-interest, highly secure bonds issued by large companies or even the government. Some of these bonds are limited to how much you can invest during a specific period, such as I-bonds (part fixed interest rate, part inflation-adjusted rate), but generally, you are free to invest as much as you please. So, for a conservative option, these are generally a great investment.

To restate, there are three bond credit quality classification categories, or more simply, **bond credit ratings**. I already touched upon junk bonds. They carry the most risk, but if you want to try your luck with them, have at it within reason.

The more legitimate bond versions are investor-grade bonds and high-yield bonds.

Researchers have determined that **investment-grade bonds** are a safer investment with less risk. However, there is always a trade-off: lower risk comes with lower interest on the money you loaned out.

High-yield bonds carry more risk than investment-grade bonds, but at the same time, can provide a higher return on investment.

This is why many advisors I know recommend that young people take a more aggressive investment approach, tailored to their circumstances, goals, and risk tolerance. Then, investing more conservatively is recommended later in life, especially for many of our retired clients. It's a great opportunity to shoot your money with "B12 shots" of aggressive growth and then protect it with conservative strength later.

Exchange Traded Funds (ETF)

According to Investopedia:[5]

Exchange-Traded Fund (ETF)

a: a type of pooled investment security that holds multiple underlying assets, rather than only one.

An ETF is a group of stocks and bonds that an investment management firm manages. Some popular firm names include BlackRock, Vanguard, WisdomTree, Fidelity, Invesco, and Direxion. While these companies offer a wide range of products and services (Fidelity, for example, serves as our clients' current custodian), one of their key sectors includes creating and managing ETFs. However, the emphasis on ETFs may vary between firms.

They are a simple concept. ETFs are a straightforward investment concept. The majority are passively managed, meaning they track an index like the S&P 500®. However, professional managers actively manage some ETFs by selecting stocks or bonds to achieve specific goals, bundling them under one name. What is the benefit, you may ask? Why not invest in a bunch of stocks myself?

Well, you can, though that approach may be limiting because the stocks within the ETFs are specified, selected, and, depending on the focus of the fund, many are already diverse. There is nothing wrong with soloing it but remember that it is the fund manager's job to stay on top of the fund's performance, which might mean adjusting the asset mix.

There is an ETF for anything. You can explore options on platforms like Morningstar, Yahoo Finance, or even by doing a quick Google search. There are over nine thousand ETFs to choose from.[6] This gives you a wide range of options. Many can help you diversify your investments, but keep in mind that not all ETFs are broad-based, some target single industries or trends.

---

[5] James Chen. Investopedia. April 29, 2025. "Exchange-Traded Fund (ETF): What It Is and How to Invest" https://www.investopedia.com/terms/e/etf.asp

[6] State Street Global Advisors. 2024."ETF Impact Report 2024-2025: The Next Wave of Innovation" https://www.ssga.com/library-content/assets/pdf/emea/equities/2024/spdr-etf-impact-report-2024-2025.pdf

Investing in an ETF will split your money within a category or industry under the given list and description. Imagine you have an eCommerce ETF. That would feature Google, Amazon, Temu, Alibaba, Wayfair, Etsy, Home Depot, Walmart, Target, Staples, and Apple, just for the sake of this example.

Imagine if the sitting U.S. president slapped tariffs so hard on Chinese e-commerce companies and their imports that it scared the living daylights out of them. By "tariff," I mean a tax on import/export goods. Which companies are going to struggle? Alibaba and Temu. Those are Chinese companies known for their direct-from-factory ordering process and wide variety of extremely cheap goods. When such events happen, companies and their shareholders can lose a lot of money.

Imagine if you had only invested in a couple of companies, such as Temu and Alibaba, without the management of an advisor or at least the ETF. You could lose a substantial amount of money. Luckily, you went a different route, and that's not your reality. You bought the ETF. This way, your losses aren't tied to just a few companies; your results depend on a broad range of them.

Not only are there trade-offs in the investment world but also checks and balances. ETFs are a great investment tool, but like anything created, they have flaws. They cover categories and industries, so imagine what might happen to an ETF if an industry struggled, rather than just a single company. In such cases, the ETF's performance would suffer, and so would your investment.

That said, industries are generally more difficult to disrupt than individual companies. Still, major events like accidents, shortages, or regulations can cause substantial effects. Additionally, ETFs come with costs, such as purchase expenses or ongoing management fees. Thoroughly research these fees and understand the funds before investing, or consult a financial advisor.

Many ETFs are actively managed, which means underperforming or risky stocks can be replaced with others when needed. For instance, in our example, significant trade restrictions or tariffs might prompt the removal of two Chinese e-commerce companies and their replacement with different stocks. This environment could create challenges for companies like Alibaba and Temu unless they adapt their business strategies, such as establishing U.S. operations or shifting their focus to other markets. However, actively managed ETFs carry different risks than index based ETFs, since performance depends on the managers' investment decisions. They can outperform or underperform similar passive funds and often have higher costs.

As a final note, ETFs are tax-efficient because they use an "in-kind" creation and redemption process; however, you may still owe capital gains on more actively managed ETFs when the trade stocks within their portfolio.

Mutual Funds

Finally, we reached the last primary body of the public investment world — Mutual Funds.

According to Oxford Languages,
Mutual Fund [myoōCH(əw)əl ˌfənd]
a: an investment program funded by shareholders that trades in diversified holdings and is professionally managed.

Mutual funds are similar to an ETF in that they provide diversification. The difference is that, with a mutual fund (also called an open-end investment company), you're entrusting your money to a manager who pools it with other people's funds and invests on their behalf. Your money is pooled and overseen by a company, rather than directly buying individual stocks yourself (which is how it's similar to an ETF).

While ETFs trade on an exchange, a mutual fund combines all contributors' money, and then the organization managing the fund invests that collective money for you. When you invest in a mutual fund, you receive mutual fund "shares" representing your ownership stake in the fund's pool of assets. If you want your money back (your principal plus any gains, minus any losses and fees), you redeem those shares back to the fund company rather than selling them on a stock exchange.

Unlike stocks or ETFs, which trade throughout the day, mutual funds are priced once daily after the market closes, based on their Net Asset Value (NAV). When you place a redemption order (requesting the Mutual Fund company to buy back your shares), you'll receive the next calculated NAV if your order is submitted before the cutoff time, usually 4 p.m. EST. Settlement times for mutual fund transactions typically take one to two business days, though it can occasionally take up to three. Additionally, some mutual funds may charge redemption fees if you sell your shares within a short holding period, often thirty to ninety days, to discourage frequent trading.

Mutual funds often distribute income (e.g., dividends or interest) and capital gains. You can reinvest those distributions to buy more fund shares or have them paid out to you in cash. Regardless of your preferred distribution method, you may owe the appropriate tax on that income.

That was a lot to take in, but it's a great advantage! The variety of options and details means you have plenty of flexibility with your money. This diversity opens the door to strategic wealth-building opportunities and lets you grow your investments in many different ways. While these are some of the most common and foundational investment vehicles, they only scratch the surface of investment opportunities. You're not stuck with one route; you can do all, more of one, or all in one investment vehicle. Everyone is different. Personally, I like stocks and ETFs. Your priority is to do what suits you and your needs.

The Executive Summary

In summary, here are the takeaways from this chapter.

The concept of public investment originated from the Dutch East India Company in 1602. This organization introduced the idea of a public sharing system, democratizing investments across all classes. Four common investment vehicles are widely used in the financial world: stocks, bonds, ETFs, and mutual funds. While these are popular options, they represent just a portion of the many asset types available to investors. Each carries risk and potential benefits, tailored to different investor needs and timelines.

Stocks

Stocks represent a share in the ownership of a company and its profits or losses. Investing in stocks means engaging in the market's volatility, which can offer significant returns but comes with higher risk.

Bonds

Bonds are generally safer investments that provide fixed returns, representing a loan from the investor to a corporation or government. While less volatile, they offer lower returns than stocks but are a staple for conservative portfolios.

ETFs (Exchange-Traded Funds)

ETFs allow investors to buy into a diversified portfolio of assets. Professionals manage them by adjusting holdings to optimize performance, offering a balance between the hands-on management of mutual funds and the flexibility of stock trading.

Mutual Funds

Similar to ETFs in diversity, mutual funds pool money from multiple investors to purchase a wide array of securities. Managed by professionals, they are ideal for those who prefer hands-off investments but want to benefit from a diversified portfolio. They are tax-efficient investment vehicles as opposed to buying and selling multiple stocks, as you would have to pay taxes on each sale.

Investment Strategies

The choice between aggressive and conservative investments should align with your stage in life, financial goals and risk tolerance. Younger investors may benefit from taking on more risk with aggressive stocks or ETFs, while older investors might prefer the stability of bonds and conservative mutual funds. I will cover these strategies in greater detail later.

CHAPTER 4

Speculation vs. Investing:
The Misunderstood Divide

"The stock market is designed to transfer money from the impatient to the patient."
~ Warren Buffett

I f you've ever heard someone say, "investing is just legal gambling," you're not alone. That myth is everywhere — especially among young people who see headlines about GameStop, crypto spikes, or overnight millionaires. But here's the truth: **Investing and speculation are not the same thing.** And understanding the difference could mean the difference between building real wealth and watching your money vanish in a flash.

When you invest, you're putting your money behind something that creates value over time. When you speculate, you place a bet that someone else will pay you more later — without always knowing *why* they would.

What Is Investing?

Investing is about **ownership** and **value creation**. It means buying a piece of something — like a business — that you believe will grow, produce value, and reward you over the long term. When Warren Buffett invests, he doesn't just buy a ticker symbol. He buys into a company that he understands and makes sense to him. He studies how that business earns money, what gives it an edge over competitors, how strong its leadership is, and whether its mission aligns with long-term success.

John C. Bogle, the founder of Vanguard, championed the idea that investing isn't about trying to outsmart the market. It's about **owning the market**. Through low-cost index funds, Bogle taught generations that they could build wealth steadily by sharing in the overall economy's growth.

Peter Lynch, legendary manager of the Fidelity Magellan Fund, believed in investing in what you know. He urged investors to look for companies they understood — businesses whose products they used and trusted, and whose value they could explain in plain English. Lynch made investing approachable by showing that solid research and common sense often beat hype and complexity.

What Is Speculation?

Speculation is about **price movements**. It focuses on predicting where prices will go next rather than on the value of what's behind those prices. When you speculate, you're hoping to profit from short-term market swings. You're essentially betting that you can time things right. Speculation often looks like this:

- **Buying** a stock, cryptocurrency, or other asset because it's suddenly popular — not because you understand its value.
- **Jumping in** on a news headline, thinking you can ride a wave before it crashes.
- **Trading frequently**, hoping to capitalize on volatility.

Speculation isn't inherently bad — but it's important to recognize it for what it is: higher risk, shorter term, and more dependent on timing and luck than solid fundamentals.

My Journey: From Tickers to Companies

When I first started investing, I'll be honest — I focused on ticker symbols and trends. I'd follow the news and look for price swings, hoping to jump on a stock after good news or a dip from bad news. It felt exciting, and sometimes it paid off in the short term.

But the more I learned, the more I realized that real, lasting success wasn't in chasing headlines. It was in **understanding businesses**. I began to focus on companies that had something enduring: a mission I believed in, strong leadership, ethical practices, and products or services that people truly needed. I looked at how they treated employees and customers, how they planned for the future, and whether they had a durable edge.

That shift in mindset made me a better investor. Long-term investing — owning a piece of a company and letting time work in my favor — suited me far more than reacting to short-term market noise. It's not about catching the next big thing. It's about building something that lasts.

The Key Differences: Investing vs. Speculation

	Investing	Speculation
Focus	Value creation, ownership	Price movements, timing
Time Horizon	Long term (years, decades)	Short term (days, weeks)
Mindset	Business owner	Trader or bettor
Risk Level	Managed, measured	Higher, often less predictable
Goal	Grow wealth steadily	Profit from price swings

When Speculation Has a Place

Speculation isn't always wrong. There's room for it — but only if you know the game you're playing and use money you can afford to lose.

Speculation can teach valuable lessons about risk and market behavior. Separating your speculative capital from your serious, long-term investments is key.

Building Your Investing Philosophy

If there's one thing I hope you take from this chapter, it's that patience and purpose win over time. Follow the guidance of investors like Buffett, Bogle, and Lynch. Think like a business owner. Invest in what you understand. Stay focused on long-term goals. And remember that slow and steady really does win the race.

Final takeaway

Don't confuse motion for progress. The patient investor wins the long game.

CHAPTER 5

Curiosity Killed the Investor

I'd like to address real questions asked by people I know and good friends of mine in and around my age group. If you have any questions, do not hesitate to email me. I'll do my best to get back to you.

Here are some great questions from my friends. Many of these were asked by multiple people, so hopefully, I'll answer some of your personal questions as well. Please remember — this is not personalized investment advice. Rather, these are general principles that may or may not be applicable to your personal situation.

From my buddy Ronald…

Question: "Can you help me understand how to invest in myself and maintain order in my finances? I am a young adult worry about these things."

Response: Why worry about it? Think a little more positively, Ronald.

Seriously! Taking advantage of this opportunity can lead to large savings in the long run. Ronald should consider educating himself — like you, the reader, are doing — and not shy away from talking to people or conducting research. Keep in mind, however, that search results will vary, and some people's passion and expertise will differ. I strongly dislike it when someone says, "Just put your savings in a couple of large stocks and aggressive ETFs." This approach can come across as lazy and apathetic. Adopting that mindset could potentially lead to significant financial losses and reduced protection. While simplicity can be beneficial in some cases, it has drawbacks, especially in more complex situations.

One of the best ways to invest in yourself (when it comes to investments) is by developing positive financial habits. When clients of Kelly Financial come bearing good habits, that makes the adviser extremely happy, especially for their future success. Do not hesitate to regularly allocate some of your saved or unspent money into certain assets on a weekly, monthly, or yearly basis. By doing this habitually, you'll allow your money to compound over time, and eventually, those compounded returns will work in your favor. Remember: buy low, sell high, and hold your positions during market stress.

FYI … Compounding is the process in which the earnings on an investment generate their own earnings. Over time, this effect accelerates the growth of investments, making early and regular contributions incredibly powerful. My father drilled this important tool and piece of knowledge into my sister's and my brains. As you mentioned, Ronald, this is the essence of investing in yourself.

To maintain order in your finances, refer to chapter 2. Track your expenses regularly to help ensure you aren't overspending, and practice self-discipline. Order stems from cultivating orderly habits and making thoughtful choices. You can still enjoy coffee, beer, or whatever you like in college. Eating out and buying clothes are fine as long as you keep it under control. It's possible to enjoy life while building savings and investing in the market.

Question: "Do you think it's worth attending a top-tier college if it means going into debt? Would taking an extra year of high school (if my school offers this) and investing in myself to see how far I can go be beneficial — especially when it comes to improving my chances for financial aid?"

Response: It depends. You should make some decisions. What kind of job are you aiming for? College might not always be necessary if you're considering a career in social services, the military, a blue collar profession, or a trade. On the other hand, if you're interested in playing sports at a collegiate level, pursuing a career that requires specialized education, working in academia, or entering a field that typically values a degree, college could be worth exploring. Ultimately, it depends on your goals and what feels right for you.

However, when you have the opportunity to save money, please take it. For example, if you think spending the first two years of college learning the same general education as Harvard University isn't worth the hefty price tag (and I frankly don't think it is), consider starting at a community college. You'll pay significantly less in tuition — or even nothing at all in certain states (for residents of that state).

I understand there is pressure to go straight to a four-year college. But let me be blunt: the system is flawed. The education isn't the problem — it's the price tag. Colleges often overcharge for the value of what they're offering, and I'm confident you see where I'm coming from. You'll receive the same Gen Ed as you would at Brown, Rutgers, Purdue, or Providence College.

If you land a fantastic scholarship, that's a different story — it solves your financial worries. But the key takeaway is simple: **don't spend money where you don't need to.**

If you can live like that, I guarantee you will be better off financially than if you don't. I am not preaching a revelation; it's common sense. Yet many in my generation make costly mistakes, such as racking up massive debt.

That is my baseline thought process, but I understand that it's not always as black and white as it seems. Ultimately, the choice is yours. If you can avoid debt at all costs, do it. If you can save money by doing a post-grad year, go for it. If you can save money by playing sports, give it a shot. But if you don't need it, don't bother. Focus on your dreams.

A college degree is important in the working world, but it's not everything. I know this firsthand. One of the most talented advisors at our company "only" has his associate's degree, yet he is a brilliant advisor and high performer. If you met him, you'd likely assume he holds a master's degree in our industry. And frankly, at his level of knowledge, he might as well have one. His success comes from his persistence, knowledge absorption, and high-drive **passion**. He's happy, folks. School wasn't for him, and that's okay — because different, and often better paths await some people.

What's his secret? He works hard, takes the time to learn, stays true to himself, and *most importantly,* **has fun.** Bill Gates once remarked, quoting Charles J. Sykes, "Your school may have done away with winners and losers, but life hasn't." And that's exactly why persistence, self-learning, and passion are so important. Life is the ultimate teacher, and success often comes to those who embrace its lessons, no matter their educational background.

Given that, here's my final answer: **weigh your options.**

From many people ...

Question: "Where do I even start?"

Response: Great question. Download a brokerage app or set up one online on your laptop or PC. This process is for you to purchase and sell securities.

Avoid downloading the popular, flashy, or trendy brokerage apps you hear about. In my opinion, many of those apps may offer user-friendly and simplistic options that are great for new investors, but they significantly restrict and limit access to the full range of investment products available. That's a significant drawback. These platforms are notorious for outages, poor customer service, and charging higher fees for payment for order flow.

Some apps have faced lawsuits for misleading users on investment decisions. Regulators, lawmakers, and the public have also scrutinized them for gamifying investing — making it seem more like a game than a serious financial decision.[7] And even though you might say, "Okay, that's just harsh criticism," take a minute to reflect. When dealing with assets that:

- Require careful, frugal, and deliberate handling, and

---

[7] Maggie Fitzgerald. CNBC. March 31, 2021. "Robinhood gets rid of confetti feature amid scrutiny over gamification of investing"
https://www.cnbc.com/2021/03/31/robinhood-gets-rid-of-confetti-feature-amid-scrutiny-over-gamification.html

- Could significantly impact your financial future if mismanaged,

it's worth considering whether such platforms are the best choice for your investments.

Would you prefer an app that feels like a game, encouraging impulsive behavior, or a serious financial service that promotes thoughtful decision making? You may prefer a classic brokerage firm. That said, the modern and trendy apps are still out there, and if you set your heart on using something like that, don't let my words discourage you. At the end of the day, it's your choice — do what feels right for you.

If you choose to do business with traditional brokerage investment firms the positives may outweigh the negatives. These firms offer a broader — if not complete — array of investment options. They are well established, with sophisticated investment vehicles and access to international markets. You'll benefit from stronger customer support (which has improved since the pandemic), advanced trading platforms, educational resources like webinars, tutorials, and classes, a high level of security, no commission fees, and cash management features, to mention a few. Your options are far superior, and the level of customization available is leagues ahead of modern, trendy apps.

However, this does come with a trade-off: ease of use. The platforms can feel less user-friendly and more intimidating, especially for those new to investing. But here's what I must say: **Don't be nervous.** These services work, and there's a way to figure everything out. Take the time to learn and practice. Don't be afraid to click on things, look up questions, or even call their support team — I have done so before, and they're invaluable.

If you're still struggling, reach out to a financial professional. That's what they're there for — and so much more.

Use these companies to begin purchasing your first investments and assets. Explore, experiment, and approach it confidently — there's no need for fear. This step marks the beginning of an exciting new chapter in successful planning and decision making for your future. Congratulations, my friend.

Question: "What's a good routine to help me balance the fun and responsibilities of college life?"

Response: Start by mastering the basics.

Set clear goals for yourself. For instance, say, "I'm going to make it a goal to invest this much of my money into the market. I'll allocate my investments across these types of assets. I will also keep an eye on my spending, save enough to have fun, and save enough to invest in the market." By adopting this mindset and doing your homework on investing, you can strike a healthy balance. If you stick to this approach, I see no reason you can't graduate with significantly more money than you started with while thoroughly enjoying the experience, assuming you are not in debt, and tuition does not enter this equation.

When Warren Buffett was around eight years old, he would ride his bike to gas stations, "scooping bottle caps out of the wells beneath the ice chests where they had fallen after customers popped their sodas open," according to his biographer, Alice Schroeder.[8] He would count the caps, sort them by brand, and use this information to determine which soda brands were the most popular in his community.[9]

Warren, of course, went on to do pretty well for himself. For those who may not know, Warren Buffett is one of the world's most successful and well-known investors and served as the Chairman and CEO of Berkshire Hathaway through 2025.[10] His story is fascinating and inspiring, showing how his early experiences shaped the man he is today. If you haven't yet explored his life story, it's worth reading.

---

[8] Jeff Cunningham. Medium. July 30, 2023. "The Birthplace of Inspiration" https://medium.com/states-of-grace/the-omaha-ethos-inside-the-mind-of-warren-buffett-6eabef4a288c

[9] Lindsay Ekstrom. LX Artworks. April 24, 2024. "Warren Buffet's First Investment" https://lxartworks.com/blogs/blog/warren-buffets-first-investment

[10] Brian Baker. Bankrate. June 20, 2024. "Who are the top executives at Berkshire Hathaway?" https://www.bankrate.com/investing/berkshire-hathaway-executives/

This question comes from my friend Jonny…

Question: "Besides investing in bank accounts for my retirement, what should I be doing about my finances for the future me?"

Response: Keeping money in the bank is important but can be harmful if that's all you do. The money you earn should be safeguarded in a checking or savings account, providing a secure backup for your finances. However, while saving is essential, in my opinion one of the worst things someone can do is leave all their money sitting in the bank!

My junior-high Econ teacher taught us a Bible verse, Matthew 25:14–30, where Jesus tells the story of a master who left his servants entrusted with his wealth while he went on a long journey.

Two servants use the master's money to do business and double their returns. However, the third and last servant buried his portion of the master's money. The master returns and says to the first two servants, "Well done, good and faithful servant. You have been faithful over a little; I will set you over much."

However, the third servant wasn't so lucky after his poor decision. When the master learns he buried the money and didn't do anything productive with it, he says, "You wicked and slothful servant! …you ought to have invested my money with the bankers, and at my coming I should have received what was my own with interest." And he casts the worthless servant into the outer darkness."

Yikes. Unfortunately, this happens often. Wickedness doesn't cause the situation; fear does. People often hesitate to invest their money in areas of growth that come with more risk and potential challenges. Yet, this fear can limit their ability to seize opportunities for greater returns, even within the most conservative portfolios. Please don't make the inexcusable mistake of the third servant and leave all your money in the bank to collect little interest, or worse, bury it. Instead, portion out an amount you're comfortable risking that aligns with your financial situation. Assess your level of conservatism and aggression in your investment choices. Consider reading up on the investment asset before buying, looking at its historical rate of return, and seeing if the investment is regarded as conservative or aggressive, so you know what you are dealing with.

A very unique question from my buddy Carson…

Question: "If I wanted to invest in real estate, in say, a foreign country, with no capital, how can I do that?"

Response: Without sufficient capital, it might be challenging to safely and sustainably invest in real estate. Have you considered alternative strategies to build up resources first?

My friend Carson is in a unique situation. He's studying in Switzerland at one of the world's top schools specializing in hospitality.[11] He has an amazing vision for his future business plans and a clear idea of how he wants to succeed as an entrepreneur in the hostel, hotel, and vacation industry. However, there's no quick fix or shortcut to making an intelligent and practical real estate investment without accumulating enough capital to cover at least half of a loan.

There's an exception if it's your absolute life passion and dream. Choosing to risk everything to start your own business doing what you love is, in my opinion, one of the most valuable pursuits in life. If that's truly your calling, nothing should hold you back. However, taking out a loan could tie you down for several years of your young life, creating an obligation to repay it and limiting your ability to fund yourself fully.

Loans are not inherently bad if you are well-prepared to manage them. However, at our age, many lack the financial stability, experience, or resources to handle them responsibly. I know you probably want a better answer. Frankly, real estate can be more affordable in certain countries — Italy, for example, has some surprisingly low-cost options. That said, working and saving enough cash first to reduce financial risk before purchasing would make more sense. However, buying cheap real estate in a foreign country often comes with challenges, such as:

- The area may be abandoned or underdeveloped.
- Tourism or economic activity might be minimal, limiting its business potential.

---

[11] EHL Hospitality Business School. 2025. "Awards and Rankings"
https://www.ehl.edu/en/about-ehl/awards-and-rankings

Additionally, the property might require renovation and maintenance, leading to additional and potentially significant expenses. With all that in mind, if you need capital, consider focusing on securing a good job first, saving diligently, and investing wisely to grow your funds. Set that money aside specifically for your future passion, and you'll be ready to make your move when the time is right. You got this!

This question is from my friend Jordan…

Question: "What exactly is a 401(k)?
And what is a Roth IRA?
Maybe stupid questions, but I don't know."

Response: Those are not stupid questions. In fact, they are extremely important and great questions that I will cover in the next chapter!

The Dynamic Duo, Squared

Picture this: you're lounging on a beach in Bali, sipping on a fresh coconut, or maybe you're hiking through the Swiss Alps, soaking in the crisp mountain air. Perhaps you're finally turning your side hustle into a full-time passion project or spending your days exactly how you've always dreamed, with no alarm clocks dictating your schedule. That's the beauty of retirement when you've built the freedom to live life on your terms. Right now, you might be in high school, juggling college classes, or just stepping into your first job, and retirement feels light years away. But here's the secret: the choices you make today, like starting a **401(k)** or opening an **IRA**, are the stepping stones to that dream future. It's not just about hard work over the years; it's about making your money work for you. Let's break it down and get started on the path to making this vision your reality.

As we know them today, retirement accounts came into existence around the time your parents were born (if you're part of Gen Z). Congress created and refined these accounts to address the decline of traditional pension systems, which had been a key part of American retirement planning for decades.

Because retirement accounts were still new and evolving, your parents may not have had the knowledge, access, or resources to benefit from them fully. The good news is that, over the years, these accounts have become much more streamlined. Their contribution and

41

withdrawal processes are now easier to understand and use, giving you the tools to take full advantage of them for your future.

That said, it's important to remember that these retirement accounts are products of legislation, governed by Congress and the Internal Revenue Code. This situation means the rules around them can change at the government's discretion. Staying informed and consulting with financial advisors will help you make the most of these investment opportunities and adapt to any changes.

Retirement accounts are complex and heavily driven by tax law. The last thing I want to do is bore you into oblivion, and that's not necessary. Let's focus on what we need to know today, while we're young, preparing to, or launching our careers and portfolios.

Opening a retirement account and making your first contributions might feel small, almost insignificant. You might even wonder if it's worth it to set aside that little bit of money when there are so many other things you could spend it on right now. Time and patience allow every small contribution to grow thanks to compound interest (more in Chapter 10. Compound interest is basically your money earning its own money, and then that earned money earns even more money.

The key here is starting early, as it gives your money more time to grow and multiply. Even if you can only contribute a little right now, those contributions will have decades to build on themselves and become something substantial.

Your retirement account needs a little attention, but that doesn't mean obsessively checking it every day. It just means staying consistent with your contributions and making wise decisions about investing your money. Later, when you've fast-forwarded your life a few decades, you'll have the financial security and freedom to live the life you've dreamed of after all those years of hard work.

You'll hear about two main types of retirement accounts, and they both have some pretty cool perks: **tax-deferred** and **tax-free**. Here's the deal:

- **Tax-deferred accounts** (like a 401(k) or IRA) are kind of like hitting "pause" on taxes. You don't pay taxes on the money you put in or the growth it earns *until* you take it out later, usually in retirement.

- **Tax-free accounts** (like a Roth 401(k) or Roth IRA) work differently. You pay your taxes upfront on the money you put in, but once it's in, it grows without taxes, and you get to take it all out tax-free someday. It's like paying the cover charge at the door and then enjoying unlimited free snacks inside the party.

Both are designed to help you grow your money faster. You're picking between saving on taxes now or saving on taxes later, and you win either way.

Let's deep dive into these two types of accounts.

Tax-Deferred Retirement Accounts

Tax-deferred retirement accounts, like a 401(k) or traditional IRA, are like putting your money into a secret booster mode for the future. Here's how it works, and why it's a game-changer: When you contribute to a tax-deferred account, you don't pay taxes on that money right now. Instead, your contributions come straight from your paycheck before Uncle Sam takes his cut. This strategy lowers the amount of money you're taxed on today, which means *more money in your pocket now*. It's like skipping the fee at the amusement park entrance because you're promising to pay it later when you leave.

Here's the cool part: while your money is chilling in the account, it grows without any taxes slowing it down. All the money you earn from investments (like stock growth or dividends) stays in the account and keeps growing, which means you're maximizing how much you'll have in the future. It's kind of like snowballing in a video game. Every win you rack up builds on itself until you're an unstoppable force.

When retirement rolls around, you'll eventually pay taxes on whatever you withdraw from the account. But here's the thing — that's a problem for future you, and by then, you'll likely be retired and in a lower tax bracket, meaning the taxes could hit you less hard than they would now. Essentially, you get to save and invest **more money upfront**, letting it grow bigger, before settling your tax bill later.

Why should you care in your twenties? Because getting started now is like discovering a cheat code. The earlier you start, the more time your money has to grow. Here's an example: imagine you put $100 into a 401(k) every month starting when you're twenty-one. Thanks to compound interest (and no taxes slowing down the growth), that money could turn into hundreds of thousands of dollars, or even a million, by the time you're in your sixties. Starting early is the key to unlocking all that juicy growth potential.

For most people, these accounts are tied to jobs. If your company offers a 401(k) and matches part of your contributions, it's like getting free money. Yup, **free money**. If you contribute $1, your company might throw in another $1, which is basically doubling your savings. You wouldn't leave free food at a party, so why leave free cash on the table?

Long story short, tax-deferred accounts are the ultimate "grow now, pay later" tool for making your money work harder than you. It's all about setting yourself up to win big in the future while keeping today's grind a little lighter on your wallet.

Roths

Tax-free retirement accounts, Roth 401(k) and IRAs, are the ultimate "pay now, enjoy forever" deal for your future self. Here's how they work and why they're perfect for someone in their twenties.

When you contribute to a Roth IRA, you use money you've *already* paid taxes on. That means you're doing the heavy lifting now, but here's the sweet part: once your money is in the account, it grows tax-free. Yes, tax-free! Every dollar your account earns from investments (like stocks, bonds, or even ETFs) grows without Uncle Sam taking another bite. And when you retire, you can withdraw every penny — including the gains you earned along the way — *completely free of taxes*. It's like paying for an all-you-can-eat buffet upfront and never worrying about the check, no matter how much you pile on your plate.

Here's why this is so important when you're starting out in your twenties. At this point in your life, you're probably paying less in taxes than you will later when you're making more money. Think about it like ordering concert tickets now, while prices are low, instead of waiting years when the same show costs double. By paying taxes now while your income is lower, you're locking in that tax-free status for future withdrawals, which will likely be worth much more.

Another reason these accounts are awesome? Flexibility. With a Roth account, you can withdraw the money you put in (but not the earnings) *anytime* without penalties or taxes. It's like a savings buffer with benefits. While it's better to leave the money alone so it can grow into something amazing, knowing the option is there can be a huge comfort when you're just starting out and life is unpredictable.

And the earlier you start, the more powerful a Roth can be. Here's some quick math magic for you: if a twenty-two-year-old invests $100 a month in a Roth IRA, earning an average 8 percent annual return, they could have close to $400,000 by the time they're sixty-five. That's the power of compounding combined with **zero taxes** on their growth. Starting early is like planting seeds in Stardew Valley, only to wake up to a fully bloomed farm years later. All you have to do is water it consistently (make regular contributions) to see massive results.

The only catch? There are limits to how much you can contribute each year (for 2025, it's $6,500 if you're under fifty) and income limits to qualify. But if you're eligible, a Roth IRA is one of the smartest moves you can make for future-you. It's the kind of financial glow-up that'll have your future self giving you a standing ovation in retirement.

Here's the deal: your future self is counting on you. Retirement accounts like 401(k)s and IRAs might not seem like the most exciting thing right now, but they're practical strategies for creating a future where you call the shots. We've talked about two MVPs of saving for retirement — **tax-deferred accounts**, where you hold off on paying taxes now to bank more upfront, and **tax-free accounts**, Roths, where you pay taxes now to reap tax-free rewards later. Both are like little engines that take your money and grow it into something way bigger, thanks to the magic of compound interest.

The best part? Starting early is your secret weapon. It doesn't matter if you're working part-time or still in school. Whatever you can save now will potentially snowball into something massive by the time you retire. Think of it as setting up a future where you can live on your terms, whether that means traveling the globe, pursuing your passions, or simply not stressing about money.

Here's your mission moving forward (and yes, it's totally doable): explore your options, start small, and stay consistent. Your future self will reflect on this moment and want to high-five you for being proactive. Retirement may feel a long way off, but every choice you make today shapes what your tomorrows will look like.

You've got this. Now, go plant your financial saplings, start building your wealth, and watch your dreams grow into reality. Future-you is already cheering you on!

CHAPTER 7

No Falling in the Pit

Your decisions in your late teens and twenties can set the stage for a lifetime of financial success — or a series of costly lessons. This chapter dives into the most common mistakes young investors make between the ages of eighteen and twenty-eight. By understanding these pitfalls now, you can sidestep them and build a smarter, stronger financial future. Let's explore a couple of *tales of caution*.

Emily and John were young, ambitious people, each building their careers in well-paying and bustling industries. Despite their similarities, they had very different approaches to financial decisions.

Emily started to invest around the age of twenty-five. She believed that if she began immediately in her career, or extremely early, the strategy would allow her to take full advantage of compounding and the power of time. Though she was just starting in her career and wasn't making that much money yet, she decided even small investments were a risk worth taking for the potential long-term rewards.

John, on the other hand, had a different philosophy. He started his career at the same time as Emily, but felt that to make impactful investments, he needed a more substantial income. So, he focused on saving money in the bank and advancing his career to earn a higher income. He believed that when he turned forty, he'd be ready to invest.

Little did John know he was falling prey to a common misconception.

Years go by, and today is Emily's fiftieth birthday. She has a substantial amount of money thanks to her early start, steady investing, and the power of compounding. She has accumulated far more money than she expected and can enjoy her retirement and the rest of her life on a higher level, with greater comfort and freedom.

John also turns fifty today. However, his financial situation tells a different story. Because he decided to wait to invest until his forties, high-fee funds that promised impressive returns drew him in. He frequently chased market trends and switched investments often. Sometimes, he even withdrew from his retirement account to cover expenses, ignoring sound financial habits. These actions cost him even more via penalties. By constantly pursuing the latest "best performing assets" instead of maintaining a consistent strategy, John missed out on the uninterrupted, steady growth that Emily benefited from.

Now, let me ask: Who do you want to be? Emily or John?

Here's a second story. This one is true, and to keep this person anonymous, we'll call our main character Sam, who lives in the suburbs outside of Metropolis.

Sam lived at home with his parents for a couple of years after he graduated from college. His level of independence was relatively low; he tried to keep up to date with what his friends were doing, and he developed the habits of a frequent spender. However, without rent to worry about and with the income from his latest job, he managed to save a significant amount of money. Despite his spending habits, he was surprisingly disciplined about consistently putting money aside.

This situation was great for Sam. However, he was restless to live on his own terms and decided he absolutely had to leave home. It became a primary goal and obsession for him. Fortunately, he landed a good accounting job in Metropolis. He relocated to the city and settled into a small, overpriced apartment, an everyday reality in dense, historic, and high-income areas. Sam's job covered the bills, just barely. However, he had a credit card and told himself, "I'll put the expenses I can't currently cover on the card and worry about it later."

First off, Sam, if you can't afford the expenses now, why would you make those purchases? Generally, it's best to hold off if you don't have the means to pay for something. I get that it might seem tempting, but relying on loans or credit later is far from a wise choice. Here's why:

- It simply delays a charge you can't afford now and may still struggle to pay later.
- It increases the overall expense thanks to interest piling up.
- You risk being penalized and damaging your credit score if you can't pay it off on time.

Returning to the story, Sam relied on credit for nearly everything — not only for rent but also for clothing, furniture, food, clubs, outings, and countless other expenses. The "I'll ride on the debt and pay it later" statement is probably the most destructive mindset and habit a human can have or say at our age. You know what, scratch that, truthfully, it's destructive at any age.

Sam eventually accumulated nearly **$50,000 of debt**. He didn't know any better then, and as a result, he found himself in a deep financial hole. Forced to turn to his family for help, he had to work out a repayment plan while spending even more time re-learning good borrowing habits. Rebuilding his credit score became an uphill battle, requiring strict discipline to pay everything back **on time**. He could have avoided this entire ordeal with some knowledge, self-control, budgeting, and the consistent tracking of expenses from the start. Unfortunately, it threw his life completely off balance.

Eventually, Sam managed to secure a repayment agreement with his family, paid off his debts, and began to rebuild his credit. However, in case you didn't know, rebuilding a bad credit score takes years.

Learn from Sam's mistakes. I felt terrible for him, but I'm grateful that his experience taught me a lesson worth remembering. Hopefully, it does the same for you.

CHAPTER 8

What-a Portafoglio!

As heard in a coffee shop...
"In an effort to maximize returns, the investor rebalanced her portfolio by adding equities, reducing bonds, and diversifying with alternative assets, all while monitoring liquidity and hedging potential risks."

Notice any new words I haven't talked about? The first I'd like to bring up is a word that originates from the Italian language, "portafoglio," which describes a briefcase dedicated to putting business documents in. Over time, the term evolved in English to describe a collection of investments — a **portfolio**.

Portfolios serve as the foundation for creating an organized map to guide new clients as they start their accounts with us. You'll work with a portfolio in your 401(k), IRA, or investment accounts, which is organized like a catalog to help you and your financial advisor navigate your investments effectively.

This is what I consider to be a portfolio:

A list, series, or catalog of organized investments intended to achieve the specific and unique goals of the owner, client, or recipient.

A financial portfolio is your personalized lineup of investments, tailored to your goals and priorities. It can take on countless forms, ranging from aggressive to conservative, or even a blend of both, such as semi-conservative with a majority aggressive allocation. Portfolios can focus on specific themes or sectors, such as sustainability, defense, technology, ETFs, bonds, money markets, stocks, mutual funds, or industrials. The possibilities are virtually limitless, offering flexibility to suit any investment strategy or preference.

Kelly Financial Services offers customizable and flexible plans to build your portfolio. Some financial advisors only offer rigid or pre-made portfolios. Kelly Financial Services uses a flexible approach depending on client needs. The first priority is respecting the wishes of each investor, along with how they want to invest. The Firm also has a vast library of portfolios that we can use to craft customized solutions.

Kelly Financial's goal is to help ensure your investments reflect what matters most to you. After all, your financial future deserves nothing less than a plan designed specifically for you. **In my experience, investors should never settle until they are happy!**

Portfolio 101

Now that we know the opening sentence represents a portfolio, let's take a closer look and break it down, piece by piece, to briefly explain its components.

Equities

Equities is a term we haven't used yet, but it's simple to understand. They represent ownership in a company, typically through stocks. When you own equity in a firm, it means you own a piece or percentage of that company, giving you a stake in its profits and future growth.

You can own equity in one specific company, like holding shares in a single business, or you can have a collection of equities in an account, meaning you own stocks from many companies. Equities are all about owning parts of companies — not other types of assets like bonds or real estate.

Diversification

Another well-known term in our industry, and a concept often recommended, is diversification. Diversifying your accounts means investing in various assets rather than concentrating on just one or a few.

This approach reduces risk compared to putting all your eggs in one basket. ETFs and Mutual Funds are great examples of diversified investment options because they represent a detailed and well-distributed collection of assets. Diversification is strongly recommended for long-term investing success.

Risk Tolerance

Risk tolerance is a crucial term in finance. It's common to be asked, "What's your risk tolerance?" before investing or making changes to your portfolio. Your risk tolerance reflects the level of uncertainty or potential financial loss you're comfortable handling when making investment decisions.

Volatility

Volatility refers to the degree to which an investment's value fluctuates over time. For example, TECL, a triple-leveraged ETF, is considered highly volatile due to its amplified exposure to a constantly evolving and growing industry. This EFT is considered highly volatile due to its amplified exposure to a continually evolving and growing industry. On the other hand, a less volatile option might be investing in a slow-growing, government-issued, or investment-grade bond, both of which typically offer more stability.

Capital Gains (Losses)

You may have heard all the buzz about capital gains tax (for example, in real estate) and had no idea what that meant. A capital gain (loss) is the investment realized when an asset is sold at a higher price than originally purchased.

Asset Allocation

The term asset allocation refers to the strategy of dividing a portfolio among different types of investments to balance risk and reward. For example, a portfolio might have an asset allocation of 50 percent stocks, 40 percent bonds, and 10 percent CDs. CDs (certificates of deposit) are low-risk investments similar to money market accounts but typically offer a fixed, modest interest rate.

Hedging Techniques

Hedging involves using financial instruments and strategies to reduce risk and protect against adverse market movements, providing a layer of security for investors. Common hedging tools include options and futures, which allow investors to lock in prices or limit potential losses. By mitigating downside risk, hedging can help stabilize returns and add a strategic edge to an investment portfolio.

Are you familiar with contracts? I'd be surprised if you weren't. Contracts are everywhere, whether you notice them or not. At the grocery store, for example, the price you see on a product acts as a contractual statement: "For this 12-pack of Red Bull, you pay $12 on sale." When you purchase it at the register, you agree to that contract. The receipt you receive serves as proof of the agreement, and if something goes wrong, that receipt is your evidence to resolve the issue.

Of course, that's a basic example of a contract. More complex contracts come into play in situations like renting an apartment, being employed, applying for a mortgage, purchasing a club membership, or entering into any other significant agreements. However, stock options are one type of contract that many people are less familiar with.

Stock Options

Do you want protection for your assets? A contract you can sell like a product to earn a premium? Or perhaps you want to increase the odds of success if you believe a stock is going up or down, with a built-in system that gives you the right to act on that belief? Economists created options specifically for these purposes.

An option is a contract that gives you the right — but not the obligation — to buy or sell an asset (like stock or ETF) at a specific price (known as the **strike price**) on or before a certain date.

Option contracts come in two types, defined by whether you are buying or selling.

While derivatives like options and futures can help mitigate some of the risks associated with investing in stocks, they carry additional risks and costs, and their results can vary widely depending on market conditions and strategy type. Some options strategies can expose investors to losses greater than the amount invested, and the loss potential is unlimited. Other strategies limit losses to the premium paid. No options strategy can fully protect against loss or guarantee profits.

Put Options

The first type is a put option, which gives the holder the right to sell an asset at the specified strike price agreed upon in the contract.

If you predict the asset's price will go down, buying a put option acts as a form of protection. It allows you to sell the asset at the agreed upon strike price even when its market value drops. That's extremely helpful. For example, if you purchase a market asset for $1,900, pay $50 in premiums, and the stock's value falls to $1,200, the put option lets you sell it at the strike price. This transaction nets you $650 ($1,900 - $1,200 - $50 premium). You must execute this strategy before the contract expires to realize its benefits. The contract seller (or dealer) takes on the risk in this arrangement, agreeing to cover the difference if the strike price exceeds the falling market value. Conversely, if the asset's value does not decrease significantly or rises, the dealer retains the premium, which is their gain in this scenario. Risk determines the premium costs: the less likely you are to profit, the cheaper the premium; the higher the odds of your success, the more expensive the premium becomes.

Call Options

A call option is the inverse of a put. Instead of purchasing the right to sell an asset at a set price, a call gives you the right to buy an asset at an agreed-upon price, within a specific timeframe.

Let's say I predict Google's stock will shoot up in the next few months. To act on this, I purchase a call option for Google. A week later, Google launches a revolutionary AI product, Gemini 2, essentially ChatGPT on steroids and better in every way. That's awesome, because now I:

- Can purchase Google stock at the lower, pre-agreed price (thanks to the call option), even though the current market price has skyrocketed.
- Stand to make a huge profit!

Now you might be thinking, "Why not just buy Google stock outright instead of dealing with options?" You'd be absolutely correct in thinking that way, because you could, and you'd still be fine. Options are an entirely different realm of investment tools often used in specific strategies, such as hedging (a term closely tied to protection).

I know a lot of professionals who advocate for using options, while others avoid them entirely. Think of options as a form of financial insurance — not mandatory, but an extra layer of strategy for those who understand how to use them wisely.

To remember our options a little better, think of calls like you're "calling for a price to buy pizza" and puts are "(hopefully) putting your losses into someone else's hands, by selling it to them!" A simpler, old-fashioned mnemonic device: "Call up your friend to put him down."

To fully hedge your investment in the stock market using options, you generally need to own 100 shares of a stock for each options contract. This is because one option's contract typically covers 100 shares. For example, if you're interested in Nvidia (NVDA), you could purchase 100 shares at $126.72 each. To hedge your investment, you might also choose a put option with a strike price of $105. The fee to purchase the options, known as the option premium, is $2.85 per share, or $285 total.

It's also important to ensure that the stock you choose has an active market for its options, which means there are enough buyers and sellers to make trading smooth. You can tell this by looking at the bid/ask spread — the difference between the highest price a buyer is willing to pay and the lowest price a seller is willing to accept. A narrow bid/ask spread indicates a more liquid (or active) options market.

Futures Contracts

There's another financial product similar to options, but it works differently. Instead of giving you the right without the obligation to buy or sell, it's a contract that commits you to a purchase or sale at a specific future date. This product is called a futures contract. Hedgers use futures to protect themselves from price fluctuations, and speculators use them to profit from these changes.

For example, if you're a farmer looking to hedge against a drop in the price of your crop by harvest, you might sell a futures contract agreeing to sell your corn at a fixed price in three months. Conversely, a bread manufacturer might buy a futures contract to lock in the price of wheat to protect against a rise in prices.

Derivatives

Futures and options are both types of derivatives, meaning their value is based on an underlying asset, such as the original price, for example.

Both are commonly used by hedgers, who aim to minimize risks, and speculators, who seek to profit from price fluctuations. These contracts are traded on exchanges and require premiums to be paid when purchased, much like insurance policies.

So, options and futures are two powerful tools anyone can use to bet on market movements or protect their investments. These are just a few examples of the many innovations that make the investment universe so diverse, catering to a wide range of strategies and preferences.

Swaps and Forwards

Swaps and forwards are other types of derivatives. Swaps are exchanges of financial products, purchases, or interest rates, while forwards resemble futures contracts. The key difference is that these are typically privatized agreements, often made between institutions, which means they're irrelevant to individual investors. Still, it's good to be aware of them. You might come across these terms in a news article or a YouTube video about a significant economic event, and expanding your financial vocabulary can only work to your advantage.

REITs

REITs are the last topic to cover before moving on to the next chapter. Surprisingly, many investors I've encountered either aren't familiar with this term or simply don't pay it much attention. Technically, I could have included REITs in the chapter about the extraordinary contributions of the Dutch people, but I chose not to. Why? Because while REITs share similarities with mutual funds, they're based on income-generating real estate. And since this chapter focuses on exploring "alien" options, it's a perfect fit here, dear reader.

I'll stop dancing around the term and get to the full explanation. REITs, or Real Estate Investment Trusts, are companies that own, operate, or finance income-generating real estate. Modeled similarly to mutual funds, they allow anyone to invest in portfolios of real estate assets in the same way they'd invest in stocks from other industries.

What makes REITs especially appealing is that they provide an easy route into the real estate market without buying, managing, or financing properties directly. Thanks to a regulation requiring them to distribute 90 percent of their taxable income as dividends, REITs also offer investors a steady income stream. On top of that, investing in REITs helps diversify an investment portfolio, which, in principle, reduces overall risk — all in all, not a bad asset choice.

CHAPTER 9

Whatcha See is Whatcha Get

They are the most beloved idea and system in every society in human history. Nobody ever disliked these or their representatives. Grass is black, and the sky is also green…

I understand taxes can be annoying. I've heard the classic, "I don't remember the government being there to help during my work shift." Nor do I. Nevertheless, it exists, and that's life. It's time to focus on how to work around what we can.

The government taxes almost everything private, including certain investments taxed as regular income. While many young people fall into lower income brackets, it's not uncommon for recent college graduates to start with salaries that surpass those of more experienced workers. That said, as we get older and take on more responsibility at work, higher pay often follows, making tax efficiency and education about taxes increasingly crucial as we progress in our careers. In this chapter, I aim to help you better understand taxation and how to invest tax-efficiently and keep more of what you earn.

I am not a Certified Public Accountant (CPA) and Kelly Financial Services is not a public accounting firm. Like all of the information in this book, the information in this section is provided for general educational purposes only and should not be construed as tax or legal advice. You should consult a qualified tax professional regarding your specific situation before making any financial decisions that could have tax implications.

There are three major subdivisions of taxation in the United States. You most likely understand and know of these three and their differences.

- **Federal Taxation** is a tax levied on all American citizens regardless of their state or territorial residence.
- **State Taxation** is a tax imposed on those who reside in that specific state.
- **Local Taxation** imposes itself on citizens of the city or county of residence.

Here is a list of all major forms of taxation. These are among the things you'd learn about in an accounting or tax course. Please read through them. Some may or may not apply to you necessarily but are good to know. Time to learn!

Income Taxes

These are taxes on earnings from wages, investments, businesses, and other sources.

- **Federal Income Tax**: Levied by the IRS on individuals and businesses based on income levels.
- **State Income Tax**: Most states impose their own income tax, though some (including Texas and Florida) do not.
- **Local Income Tax**: Some cities and counties impose additional income taxes (including New York City and Philadelphia).

Payroll Taxes

These are taxes withheld from wages to fund social programs.

- **Social Security Tax**: 6.2 percent on wages up to a certain threshold (employer matches this amount). This contribution is to pay into a government-funded system that guarantees income for seniors in America, and ideally, will pay into our retirement lives too.
- **Medicare Tax:** 1.45 percent on all wages (employer matches this amount), while high earners pay an additional 0.9 percent.
- **Federal Unemployment Tax (FUTA)**: Employers pay this tax to fund unemployment benefits. This contribution is to pay into a government system that aids unemployed people, usually after losing a job.

- **State Unemployment Tax (SUTA)**: Varies by state; funds state unemployment benefits.

Corporate Taxes

Taxes levied on business profits.

- **Federal Corporate Income Tax**: Currently set at a flat 21 percent for corporations.
- **State Corporate Income Tax**: Varies by state, with some states not imposing any corporate tax (such as Wyoming and South Dakota).

Capital Gains Taxes

Taxes on profits from the sale of assets such as stocks, real estate, or businesses.

- **Short-Term Capital Gains**: Taxed as ordinary income if held for less than one year.
- **Long-Term Capital Gains**: Taxed at reduced rates (0, 15, or 20 percent) if held for over a year.

Property Taxes

Taxes on real estate, land, and personal property.

- **Real Estate Property Tax**: Levied by local governments based on property value.
- **Personal Property Tax**: Some states tax vehicles, boats, aircraft, and business equipment.

Sales Taxes

Taxes imposed on goods and services at the point of sale.

- **State Sales Tax**: Varies by state (examples: California: 7.25 percent, Texas: 6.25 percent).
- **Local Sales Tax**: Some counties and cities add local taxes on top of state sales tax.
- **Use Tax**: Applied to goods purchased out of state but used within the state.

"Sin"/Disincentive Taxes

Taxes on specific goods and activities, usually meant to discourage consumption.

- **Gasoline and Fuel Taxes**: Federal and state taxes on gasoline and diesel.

- **Alcohol and Tobacco Taxes**: Higher taxes on cigarettes, beer, wine, and liquor.
- **Firearms and Ammunition Tax**: Federal tax on the sale of firearms and ammunition.
- **Luxury Taxes**: Additional taxes on high-value items such as yachts or expensive cars.

Estate & Gift Taxes

Taxes on wealth transfers during life or at death.

- **Federal Estate Tax**: Imposed on estates over a certain threshold ($13.99 million in 2025).
- **State Estate Taxes**: Some states impose additional estate taxes.
- **Gift Tax**: Applies to gifts exceeding the annual exclusion limit ($19,000 per recipient in 2025).

Inheritance Tax

Some states impose inheritance taxes, where the recipient (not the estate) pays taxes on inherited assets (examples: Kentucky, Iowa, Pennsylvania). For inheriting your family member's, close friend's, or individual's estate, you must pay a preset tax on the goods you receive from that estate.

Tariffs

Levied on imported goods to protect domestic industries or generate revenue.

Business & Self-Employment Taxes

- **Self-Employment Tax**: Covers Social Security and Medicare (15.3 percent total for self-employed individuals).
- **Franchise Tax**: A fee businesses pay for the right to operate in certain states.
- **Gross Receipts Tax**: Some states tax business revenues rather than profits.

Alternative Minimum Tax

Ensures that high-income earners pay a minimum level of tax, even after deductions and credits.

Leisure/Fun Local & State Taxes

- Tourism Taxes: Taxes on hotels, rental cars, and entertainment venues.

- Lottery & Gambling Taxes: Taxes on winnings from casinos, lotteries, and sports betting.
- Telecommunications Taxes: Taxes on phone, internet, and cable services.

If you would like that organized in an easier-to-read fashion:

Tax Type	Level	Who Pays?	Examples
Income Tax	Federal, State, Local	Individuals, Businesses	IRS income tax, state tax
Payroll Taxes	Federal, State	Employers, Employees	Social Security, Medicare
Corporate Tax	Federal, State	Businesses	21% federal tax on corporations
Capital Gains Tax	Federal	Investors	Stocks, real estate sales
Property Tax	Local, State	Homeowners, businesses	Home, land, vehicles
Sales Tax	State, Local	Consumers	Retail purchases
Excise Taxes	Federal, State	Consumers	Gas, alcohol, tobacco
Estate & Gift Taxes	Federal, Some States	Wealthy individuals	Estates over $13.61M
Inheritance Tax	State	Heirs	Iowa, Kentucky, Pennsylvania
Tariffs	Federal	Importers	Goods from foreign countries
Self-Employment Tax	Federal	Self-Employed	15.3% total for SS & Medicare
Franchise Tax	State	Businesses	Right to operate in a state
Alternative Minimum Tax	Federal	High earners	Ensures minimum tax is paid
Tourism Taxes	Local, State	Travelers	Hotel, rental car taxes
Lottery/ Gambling Tax	Federal, State	Gamblers	Casino, lottery winnings

Now that we've discussed the layout of the American tax system, let's dive into the income tax brackets.

The tax bracket system is progressive. This term means that the more income you make, the higher percentage you pay. A common thing many people don't understand right away is that the bracket you fall in doesn't mean you pay its percentage on *all* of your income. If you were in the 2025 tax bracket at 24 percent, single, making more than ≈ $104,000, you would **not** be taxed 24 percent on the entire sum of your income. Let me explain.

The first $0 to $11,925 of the $104,000 would be taxed at 10 percent. Then, the money from $11,925 up to $48,475 would be taxed at 12 percent. Continuing, the money between $48,475 and $103,350 would be taxed at 22 percent, and so on, up to your bracket at 24 percent.

So, if you made $1.00 above $197,300 (see the graph), putting that $1.00 in the 32 percent tax bracket, you would only be taxed 32 percent on that $1.00, and your one dollar floating in that bracket would turn into 68 cents after taxes.

Here is the 2025 tax bracket for reference:

2025 Tax Brackets		
Tax Rate	**Single filers**	**Married filing jointly**
10%	$0 to $11,925	$0 to $23,850
12%	$11,926 to $48,475	$23,851 to $96,950
22%	$48,476 to $103,350	$96,951 to $206,700
24%	$103,351 to $197,300	$206,701 to $394,600
32%	$197,301 to $250.525	$394,601 to $501,050
35%	$250,526 to $626,350	$501,051 to $751,600
37%	$626,351 or more	$751,600 or more

Tax Prep Services

If you don't already have a tax preparation service, here are some options to consider. These services help you organize your information and assist with filing your taxes.

The first service is the one-and-only **TurboTax**. It's currently the leading software for tax preparation and is an e-commerce company. Positively, it can take complex tax situations and handle different lifestyles, such as self-employment. If you don't feel completely assured, they offer access to tax/audit professionals. It's an interview-style process, and their customers have regarded it as a user-friendly service. Some of the downsides include higher costs than some of their competition (especially for complex tax situations) and feature upselling upgrade prompts on its service.

The also well-known **H&R Block** serves a diverse range of clientele with online and in-person services. You have the option between online and in-person, or both. They also have competitive and transparent pricing. Similar to TurboTax, they have tax/audit professionals on standby. However, the expertise level of your tax professional may vary in location, and extra fees may appear with advanced support or state returns.

Lastly, another option is **Jackson Hewitt**. They provide tax preparation services through both physical locations and online platforms, aiming to offer flexible options for clients, just like H&R Block. They offer in-office, Walmart-based (believe it or not), and online tax preparation services. They provide assistance beyond the tax season for ongoing tax needs. On the flip side, the online platform may lack some advanced features found in its competition.

Those are the three most well-known and general tax-prep services that I wanted to share with you. However, you can find local services and different firms to suit your needs. Local or independent firms may put more focused time and quality on your tax situations, especially if you're a business owner, self-employed, or want good backing.

You should use your tax-efficient accounts, like those I discussed in Chapter 6, "The Dynamic Duo, Squared," for your retirement and future. However, I neglected to mention a few tax-efficient accounts that aren't related. I'll quickly explain the HSA and 529 Plan.

HSAs

HSAs, the abbreviation for Health Savings Accounts, are tax-advantaged medical savings accounts you can use for health bills or expenses without paying taxes and are tax deductible (tax deductibility refers to expenses that can be subtracted from your taxable income, ultimately lowering the amount of income subject to taxation.

This approach means that by strategically using deductions, like mortgage interest, business expenses, medical costs, or contributions to retirement accounts, you can reduce your taxable income and pay less in taxes). Funds are medical expenses only and are withdrawn tax free. You can roll them over indefinitely, meaning there is no rush to spend from the account. Finally, you can withdraw it after age sixty-five for non-medical reasons without penalty, and the money will have the same tax treatment as a traditional IRA.

529 Plans

For education-related savings, the 529 Plan is a savings option. There are two plans: **the education savings plan** and **the pre-paid tuition plan**. The first functions like an investment account for future education costs. Investors can use funds at any eligible educational institution (K-12, college, university, vocational, or graduate school). Investment options typically include mutual funds, ETFs, and age-based portfolios. Its growth is tax-free if it is used for qualified education expenses.

The second plan allows you to lock in tuition at today's prices for future college expenses. It's typically limited to in-state public colleges but may allow conversion for private or out-of-state institutions. This option doesn't cover non-tuition expenses (like boarding and books). It's less flexible than the education savings plan but protects against tuition inflation.

A Timeless Tale

As a child, some of my most cherished family memories were our movie nights, especially when we watched Pixar films. Even now, we still enjoy them from time to time. Pixar holds a special place in the heart of most Gen Zers, and my personal favorite is *The Incredibles*. As I've gotten older and started to understand how the world works, I became fascinated by the genius behind Pixar — its storytelling, its characters, and its jaw-dropping animation. And one of the masterminds behind it all, Steve Jobs, became one of my idols.

Now, I could write an entire book about Steve Jobs — his life, his career, his quirks — but for this chapter, let's focus on one specific moment: how he structured his pay in 1997. Trust me, it's a story worth thinking over and learning about.

The Backstory: From Fired to Fabulous

Steve Jobs co-founded Apple in 1976, and the company saw early success. But by the mid-1980s, things got rocky. Jobs clashed with then-CEO John Sculley over the company's direction, and in 1985, Apple's board of directors pushed Jobs out of the company he had built. Ouch.

Jobs didn't sulk. Instead, he flexed his entrepreneurial muscle and founded NeXT Computer, Inc. that same year. Oh, and just for fun, he also bought a struggling computer graphics division from Lucasfilm, which he renamed Pixar. You might've heard of it — it went on to create *Toy Story*, the first-ever fully computer-animated film in history. No big deal.

Fast forward to 1997, Apple was in trouble — "on the brink of collapse," trouble. But Jobs had spent the last twelve years building NeXT and its groundbreaking operating system, NeXTSTEP, which Apple desperately needed. So, Apple acquired NeXT, and with it, they got Jobs back in the deal. By 2000, he was officially CEO again. Full circle, right?

The $1 CEO

When Jobs became CEO, he didn't demand a multi-million-dollar salary like most corporate bigwigs. Nope. He took an annual salary of $1—just one dollar. Why? To show his commitment to Apple's turnaround and future success. It was a bold move, but hey, that was Steve Jobs.

Jobs had sold all but one share of his Apple stock back in 1985 when he left the company. Why keep one share? So he could still attend shareholder meetings and keep an eye on things. Smart, right?

When he became CEO in 2000, his compensation included $7.5 million in stock options — a common practice for executives. But here's the kicker: Jobs didn't exercise those options right away. And that decision? Pure genius.

Showtime

Here's where Jobs impersonates Mr. Incredible and whispers to the IRS, "Showtime!" Let's break it down:

- On his $1 salary, Jobs owed the IRS a whopping max of **40 cents** in income tax. That's it.
- On his $7.5 million in stock options? He owed **zero** taxes in 2000 because he didn't exercise them. Stock options aren't taxed until you exercise them, and Jobs knew this.

And here's the cherry on top: When you eventually sell stock, the profit is taxed as **capital gains income**, which is taxed at a much lower rate than ordinary income. Jobs played the long game, and it paid off.

Lessons from the $1 CEO

The rest of Jobs' stock option story gets a little complicated, so I'll save that for a more advanced book. But for now, here are the key takeaways:

1. **Getting fired isn't the end of the world.** Jobs was forced out of the company he founded, but he didn't let it define him. Instead, he pivoted, learned, and came back stronger.
2. **Perseverance pays off.** Life has a funny way of bringing things full circle. Jobs' journey from Apple to NeXT to Pixar and back to Apple is proof of that.

Be smart about taxes.

There are plenty of legal, creative ways to reduce your tax liability. Jobs' $1 salary and stock option strategy are a masterclass in this.

So, the next time you're faced with a challenge, channel your inner Mr. Incredible. You might just save the day — or at least your financial future.

CHAPTER 10

Compound Effect

L et's talk about **compound interest** — the phenomenon often referred to as "the eighth wonder of the world," a phrase famously (though not definitively) attributed to Albert Einstein. There's a reason my father drilled this concept into us as toddlers: it's one of the most powerful forces in personal finance.

In simple terms, compound interest occurs when your money earns interest, and then that interest earns interest, and so on. Over time, this concept can transform small, consistent contributions into a mind-blowing amount of wealth. It's like planting a tiny seed that grows into a massive tree — if you give it enough time and care.

But here's the catch: compound interest can also work against you. Misuse it, and it can bury you in debt faster than expected. That's why this chapter is about breaking down the fundamentals — how compound interest works, how it applies to investing, spending, and life choices, and how to harness it to your advantage. We'll also dive into some real-world examples to help connect the dots.

The Clean, Fluffy Snowball

Compound interest is when your principal (the amount of money you put in) earns interest, and then that interest starts to earn interest, and so on. It's a snowball rolling downhill — small at first but growing larger with every revolution.

Here are the key differences:

- **Simple interest**: Earn interest only on the principal.
- **Compound interest**: You earn interest on the principal **and** on accumulated interest.

Let's break it down with an example: Imagine you deposit $1,000 into an account with a 10 percent annual interest rate.

- Year 1: You earn 10 percent of $1,000, which is $100. Now you have $1,100.
- Year 2: You're earning interest on $1,100 instead of just $1,000. So 10 percent of $1,100 is $110. Now you have $1,210.
- Year 3: You earn 10 percent on $1,210, which is $121. That brings your total to $1,331.

See how it snowballs? Each year, your money grows faster because you're earning interest on a bigger amount. That's the magic of compound interest — it rewards patience and consistency. The earlier you start, the more time your snowball has to grow.

Keep in mind, our example doesn't factor in additional deposits. Now, imagine adding regular contributions — like with a 401(k) or other investment accounts. With those extra deposits, the power of compound interest really kicks into high gear, and your savings can grow even faster.

If there's one thing I'd scream from the rooftops about compound interest, it's this: **the earlier you start, the bigger the payoff.** Time is the MVP when it comes to letting compound interest work its magic.

- **Starting at age twenty vs. thirty**: A person who puts away just $100 a month at age twenty can often accrue *significantly* more money by retirement than someone who starts at age thirty and tries to "catch up" with bigger monthly deposits. It's a weird quirk of compounding: early money puts on the most weight.
- **Patience is key**: Compound interest is not a "get rich quick" hack — it's a "build wealth steadily over time" strategy. Give it ten, twenty, or thirty years, and you'll see the

magic unfold. The longer you let it simmer, the better it works.

When you think about investing — whether in stocks, bonds, ETFs, mutual funds, or even real estate — compound interest is the underlying engine that powers the long-term growth.

- **Reinvesting Dividends**: Some companies pay dividends to shareholders when you own their stock, especially preferred stock (as mentioned earlier in the Never Forget the Dutch chapter). By using those dividends to buy more shares, you're essentially building a bigger stockpile. And here's the magic: the next dividend payout will be based on your larger number of shares, which means even more dividends. This effect is compounding in action — your money is making money, and you're using that money to buy even more money-making shares. It's like a financial feedback loop that keeps getting stronger.

- **Compounding Capital Gains**: If you hold onto your investments long enough, you'll also see the snowball effect from rising share prices (assuming you picked solid companies or diversified wisely). You can sell off your gains to buy other stocks or let them ride and keep growing. Either way, the growth feeds on itself, like a snowball rolling downhill, picking up more snow as it goes. The longer you stay invested, the bigger that snowball can get.

- **Drip, Drip, Drip**: Many brokerage firms offer a DRIP (Dividend Reinvestment Plan). A DRIP automatically reinvests your dividends to buy additional shares — no extra effort required. If you're investing for the long haul, especially for retirement, letting a DRIP do the heavy lifting is one of the easiest ways to harness the power of compounding. It's like setting your investments on autopilot while you focus on other things, knowing your money is quietly working overtime for you.

Debt's Snowball: Packed with Sticks, Grass, and Grime

Compound interest is a powerful tool, and when used wisely, it can work wonders for your financial future. You have the power to control how it's used and to make it work for you. But let's be real — I wouldn't be doing my job as your financial guide if I didn't warn you about the flip side. Like most things in life, compound interest has downsides when working against you.

Some types of debt — like credit cards and certain loans — use compounding to their advantage, not yours. When you carry a balance, interest charges start piling up, and if you don't pay it off, you could end up paying interest on *those* interest charges. Try soothing that sting.

- **Credit Card Balances**: The classic example is letting your credit card balance spiral out of control because you only pay the monthly minimum. This process creates a vicious cycle, especially if you keep swiping your card for new purchases. The interest doesn't just vanish — it stacks up, and before you know it, financial quicksand has you in its grips.

- **Student Loans**: There are many types of student loans. Direct unsubsidized federal loans start accruing interest the moment you take them out. If you don't pay that interest while in school, it capitalizes into the principal. Suddenly, you owe interest on the interest. Fun times.

- **Payday Loans**: These borderline predatory products are the financial equivalent of a bear trap. With sky-high interest rates, they're designed to keep you stuck. Compounding interest can turn a small loan into a massive financial headache if you can't repay the loan promptly. Avoid them; otherwise, you're in for a world of hurt thanks to compounding.

The Bottom line: Compound interest is a double-edged sword. It can boost you into the stratosphere if you harness it wisely or bury you alive in debt if you let it get out of control. The key is to use it to build wealth, not as a weapon against your finances. Be intentional, stay informed, and always keep compounding on your side.

The Story of Alex and Bailey

- **Alex** starts investing $200 a month at age twenty-five into a retirement account with an 8 percent annual return. By age sixty-five, Alex has a jaw-dropping amount.
- **Bailey** waits until thirty-five to start investing that same $200 a month at the same 8 percent annual return. By sixty-five, Bailey's total is significantly less than Alex's (hundreds of thousands less). Bailey might still have a nice chunk saved, but nowhere near Alex's pile of gold. Ten extra years of compounding made a massive difference.

Here's a table comparing Alex and Bailey's retirement savings over time.

Age	Alex's Savings (Starts at 25)	Bailey's Savings (Starts at 35)
25	$0	$0
35	$36,589	$0
45	$125,349	$36,589
55	$318,670	$125,349
65	$894,646	$407,734

Takeaways:
- By starting at twenty-five, Alex ends up with $894,646 by age sixty-five.
- Bailey, starting ten years later at thirty-five, ends up with $407,734 — less than half of Alex's total.
- Those ten extra years of compounding give Alex a $486,912 advantage.

The Compound Interest "Snowball"

I've mentioned a snowball a couple of times regarding compound interest. What exactly does that mean? Put on your scarf and mittens momentarily — we're building a snowman.

1. Pack together a small snowball (your principal).
2. Roll it around the snow-covered ground (annual interest).
3. The original snowball picks up more snow (your interest grows the principal).
4. You keep rolling it in new snow patches (annual contributions).
5. The snowball becomes a giant, unstoppable force that crushes any puny snowman in the vicinity.

Alright, maybe that's a goofy metaphor, but you get the picture.

Life Imitates Art

Compound interest isn't limited to money. Some people like to talk about how certain life choices "compound" over time.

- **Skills**: If you consistently learn new things, like taking an online class, practicing an instrument, or honing a technical skill, the knowledge stacks on itself. That boost in personal growth can lead to better career opportunities, which can mean more money, which you can then invest, creating a nice feedback loop.

- **Health**: Tiny daily habits compound over time. Eating 300 more calories than you burn each day can slowly lead to weight gain, just like going for a twenty-minute run daily can improve your cardio, mood, and overall physique. The consistent "small changes, big difference" concept is another form of compounding.

- **Relationships/Networking**: The more you build trust, help people, and expand your circle, the more opportunities come your way. Think of it like growing interest on your kindness. Sappy, sure, but it's real: goodwill often cycles back to you in surprising ways.

Compound interest is not a magic wand that erases problems. It's not going to fix irresponsible spending or chronic financial negligence. You still need to:

- **Budget and Track**: Keep an eye on your cash inflows and outflows. Know exactly how much you can afford to invest each month without starving or falling into the trap of credit card debt. If you're unsure how much you're spending on those random fast-food runs or impulse buys, start by tracking your expenses meticulously for a month or two. This simple habit can give you a clear picture of where your money is going and help you make smarter financial decisions.

- **Stay Consistent**: The power of compounding works best when you invest regularly and don't yank your money out at the first sign of market turbulence or chaos. The markets will have ups and downs — that's normal. Economists refer to this as the "business cycle," which includes periods of growth and contraction as part of the economy's natural rhythm. Stick to your plan.

- **Reinvest Your Earnings**: Whenever possible, reinvest your dividends, interest, or capital gains if long-term growth is your goal. Sure, you might eventually want to take distributions in retirement, but the key to maximizing your financial snowball is to keep feeding it at every opportunity. The more you reinvest, the faster your wealth can grow, thanks to the power of compounding.

- **Avoid Unnecessary Debt**: If it's not helping you build wealth — like a reasonable mortgage or a small student loan for a career you're passionate about — it's likely just dead weight on your finances. High-interest debt is the ultimate enemy of compounding (unless, of course, you're the credit card company). Keep your focus on debt that serves a purpose and avoid letting interest work against you.

The Rule of 72

There's a concept called the "Rule of 72". It's a method to approximate how many years it will take for your money to double at a given interest rate. Simply divide seventy-two by the annual interest rate.

- If your account yields 8 percent, then 72 ÷ 8 = 9 years to double.
- If your account yields 6 percent, then 72 ÷ 6 = 12 years to double.

This rule doesn't factor in monthly contributions or compounding frequency exactly, but it's a quick mental estimate to see how powerful compounding can be, even over just a decade. As a quick summary, compound interest is your greatest ally when you start early and nurture it consistently.

However, it can quickly become your worst nightmare if you only experience it through overdue credit card bills or bad loans you can't pay off. The same unstoppable force that can catapult you to financial freedom can just as easily drag you straight to the bottom.

If you ask me, the choice is simple: harness compound interest to grow your investments and steer clear of letting it bury you in debt. The formula is straightforward: start investing early, reinvest your gains, avoid high-interest credit traps, and give your money the time it needs to grow.

And if you haven't started yet, don't panic — it's never too late. As the saying goes, "The best time to plant a tree was thirty years ago. The second-best time is today." That's some solid advice straight from my father.

Compound interest is waiting, **ready to either build you up or break you down**. The direction it takes is entirely up to you.

Key Takeaways

- Compound interest = interest on interest. Over time, it drives exponential growth.
- The younger you start, the more dramatic the results.
- It can either build your wealth or magnify your debt.

- Regular investments, reinvesting earnings, and staying disciplined are the keys to maximizing gains.
- Over time, skills, health, and relationships also benefit from a compound effect (a nod to Darren Hardy's book).
- The **Rule of 72** is a handy math trick for estimating how long it takes to double your money.

Consider this your nudge to set up an account that allows your contributions to compound, whether manually or automatically. Your future self will thank you.

CHAPTER 11

Time Has Come Today

The Chambers Brothers, a soul and psychedelic rock band from the 1960s, are best known for their hit song *Time Has Come Today*. The group of four brothers — George, Willie, Lester, and Joe — started out singing gospel in Mississippi before blending soul, blues, and rock to create a sound that captured the spirit of their era. Their music often reflected themes of change, freedom, and the consequences of life's choices.[12]

In their iconic song, the lyrics tell the story of a young person grappling with the weight of time and the consequences of their decisions. The song portrays someone who has lost their direction, left wandering without a sense of stability or a place to call home. It's a cautionary tale, a reminder that our choices today — especially regarding money and debt — can shape our future in ways we might not expect.

For Gen Z, the message is clear: don't let poor financial decisions leave you feeling like the protagonist of this song — adrift, unmoored, and without a plan.

Avoiding debt, managing it wisely, or taking precautions is ideal. However, many people my age don't realize this, lack the patience, or simply need the money. I dedicate this chapter to those who find themselves deeply in debt. My goal is to provide you with a clear and

---

[12] Jeff Tamarkin. Best Classic Bands. 2025. "When the Chambers Brothers' 'Time' Had Come." https://bestclassicbands.com/chambers-brothers-time-9-20-17/

practical road map to help you work through your debt, so you can successfully navigate your way out.

Debt Categories

There are two types of debt in my opinion: good debt and bad debt. A good friend of mine explained it this way during a conversation between the two of us:

"Look, a mortgage is what I call good debt because it's tied to an asset, and inflation works in your favor over time. Your mortgage payment stays the same, but your income should go up, and the real cost of that debt goes down. So there's no real point in throwing extra money at it —pay it off as scheduled, granted, the rate on your mortgage is LOWER than the current inflation rate.

"Now, credit card debt? That's bad debt. Those interest rates will eat you alive. If you've got a balance, a one option is a balance transfer — get a card with 0 percent interest for a while and move your balance over. Just be careful; if you don't pay it off before that promo period ends, they'll hit you with all the interest you were avoiding. You need to be smart. However, DO NOT make this a habit. Relying on balance transfers repeatedly can lead to a cycle of debt that's hard to break."

To boil it down, a mortgage you acquire may take ten to thirty years to pay off. Historically, the value of the dollar decreases over time. Remember your parents talking about how a Coke used to cost 25 cents when they were kids, and now it's $1.50? That is inflation at work. If you have a fixed cost on your mortgage, why pay it off as early as possible while your money is still worth more in dollar value than in the future? If $100,000 has way less value twenty years from now, you'd want to pay that off later than sooner — as slow as possible. (If you pay it on time and consistently, you will also help your credit score.) You also have an asset backing up that mortgage: the actual house. Pay off your mortgage slowly, so that more of your money can work elsewhere and grow.

Credit card debt is generally considered a form of unfavorable debt. It's easy to acquire. There are strategies to avoid it. The aforementioned temporary credit cards with 0 percent interest can be acquired (depending on your credit), and you can transfer your debt to these without carrying over the interest. Like my friend said, you must pay it off before the end date. While you're at it, consider finding a side gig to make money to help pay off your credit card obligation. Any money you earn in addition to your income, such as bonuses or tax refunds, should **immediately go toward your credit card debt** before anything else. At this stage of your life, additional income is one aiding vehicle to a debt exit strategy. Do not spend your bonus for fun; you cannot prioritize that.

Do you spend time on Instagram, Facebook, or YouTube? If so, you may have seen different financial influencers give financial advice over the phone or other mediums while someone either asks what to do with their ginormous fortune or insurmountable debt. They generally teach two methods for paying down debt.

The first method is the **avalanche method**, which financial guru Ramit Sethi often explains.[13] This method recommends paying off the highest interest debt first, then moving down the list.

The second method, advocated by Dave Ramsey and Ramsey Solutions, is the **snowball method**.[14] Pay off the smallest balance first for a quick and psychological win. Then roll that payment into the next one.

The best method is either. Just knock it out one at a time.

Student Loan Debt

The student loan system has become a catastrophic scheme that allows colleges, with government backing, to exploit students and their families. It has left countless young men and women financially crippled before they even begin adulthood. I know this firsthand because I've met many folks who choose a major they're passionate about — not necessarily a bank-breaking career, but one they truly love. These same people walk out of college with anywhere from $100,000 to $400,000 in debt.

As mentioned in previous chapters, if your passion doesn't require a degree, there's no shame in reconsidering college. Many colleges

---

[13] Ramit Sethi. I Will Teach You To Be Rich. December 20, 2024. "Debt Avalanche Vs Debt Snowball (Which Method Is Best For You)" https://www.iwillteachyoutoberich.com/debt-avalanche-vs-debt-snowball-method/
[14] George Kamel. Ramsey. August 19, 2025. "How the Debt Snowball Method Works" https://www.ramseysolutions.com/debt/how-the-debt-snowball-method-works?

encourage easy loans, creating incentives to charge high tuition, knowing they'll be paid—often at students' expense and with government backing.

Compared to inflation, the rise in college tuition has far outpaced regular economic inflation, making higher education increasingly unaffordable. Student loans have trapped American students in a corrupt system, accelerated and exacerbated by schools engaging in what can only be described as price gouging.

Adding fuel to the fire, many colleges employ tenured professors, meaning their job is locked in by the authority of their union, after serving as a teacher for a set number of years. While tenure can protect academic freedom, it often reduces the incentive for quality teaching. This system and increased political coercion on campuses have left many impressionable students feeling uncomfortable and confused.

On top of that, students face the burden of expensive materials (such as textbooks, which are commonly never used)[15] and are required to take unnecessary general education courses. These include subjects most people learn in high school, or mandatory, exploratory liberal arts classes that don't appeal to them or correlate with or relate to their chosen major.

I'd recommend looking at colleges abroad if this system frustrates you. Many universities overseas do not enforce these extra courses,[16] assuming you already learned those topics in high school.

Student loan debt is chaotic and overwhelming. While it is possible to default on student loans, the consequences are severe, and discharging them in bankruptcy is extremely difficult. Interest will continue to climb if you don't make payments. Also, these loans are unsecured — there are no assets backing them. Unlike a mortgage secured by a house or a car loan backed by a vehicle, a student loan lacks any tangible asset as collateral.

---

[15] Cailyn Nagle and Kaitlyn Vitez. U.S. PIRG. June 2020 "Fixing the Broken Textbook Market" https://pirg.org/wp-content/uploads/2022/07/Fixing-the-Broken-Textbook-Market_June-2020_v2-5.pdf

[16] IFSA. 2025. "5 Differences Between Uni in the US and UK" https://ifsa-butler.org/student-stories/5-differences-between-uni-in-the-us-and-uk/

Less Education For Your Buck

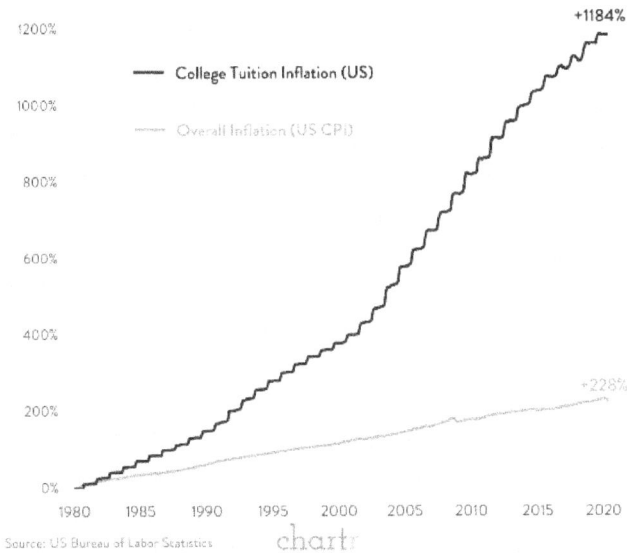

Source: US Bureau of Labor Statistics

[17]

Your best bet for tackling student loan debt is consolidation or refinancing. There's no magic fix, so please treat these as remedies instead. **Consolidation** means rolling all your student loans into one. Instead of juggling multiple payments with different interest rates, you'll have just one payment to focus on. It might even lower your monthly payment, but keep in mind it could extend your loan term — meaning you'll pay more in interest over time.

Conversely, **refinancing** involves taking out a new loan — ideally with a lower interest rate — to pay off your existing loans. This strategy can save you money over time, but it typically requires good credit and a steady income to qualify for a better rate. However, if you refinance federal loans into private loans, you'll lose access to government benefits like deferment, forbearance, and loan forgiveness programs. While refinancing can be helpful, it's not a "quick fix." You'll still need a solid plan and discipline to tackle that debt and get it off your shoulders.

---

[17] Kerby Anderson. Point of View. September 12, 2022. "Cost of College" https://pointofview.net/viewpoints/cost-of-college/

This harsh reality is why so many people emphasize avoiding debt — it can hold you back significantly. While you're busy catching up and paying off what you owe, you miss the opportunity to grow your wealth through investments. Essentially, you're pouring money into a financial void.

I understand this might have been an uneasy topic to address, but debt itself is anything but comfortable. My goal is to provide you with guidance and a straightforward strategy to navigate your way out.

For those not currently dealing with debt, consider this a warning: don't fall into a trap you can avoid now that you're informed.

Be smart — limit credit card usage, plan for college costs (like considering community college or studying abroad to save), and approach mortgages with a solid payoff strategy. The key is to stay proactive and intentional with your financial decisions. A little planning now can save you a lot of stress later.

CHAPTER 12

Show Me the Way

So, what should I actually invest in? Just tell me what to do!

I know, I've been stalling — but for good reason. You've already learned a ton about managing your finances: the basics of securities, compound interest, avoiding debt, proper saving habits, and a lot of key financial terminology. Now that you've got the foundation, it's time to dive into some real strategy.

Strategic Steps

Set up a brokerage account.

If you don't already have one, this is your starting point. There are plenty of reputable brokerage firms to choose from — Fidelity, Charles Schwab, Vanguard, and others we've discussed before. My firm's custodian is Fidelity, which is one of several large, well known brokerage and custodial firms available. If you're overwhelmed or want something simple, you could start with Robinhood. These examples are for illustration only, not a specific recommendation. Just remember the downsides and limitations we've covered earlier.

Ask yourself key questions.

Before you start investing, take a moment to reflect on these:

- What industries or fields am I interested in or familiar with?
- How aggressive or conservative do I want to be? (Hint: Investing more aggressively when you're young is generally a good idea, if your situation allows.)
- How much money am I putting in, and how much do I want to set aside for the future, with the guidance of an advisor?

That last question is crucial because it determines whether you're allocating funds to a retirement account (like an IRA, Roth IRA, or 401(k)) or a standard brokerage account. This choice significantly impacts how and when your investments are taxed and how quickly you can access your money.

Funds in tax-deferred retirement accounts are taxed upon withdrawal, often at your ordinary income tax rate, while earnings in a standard brokerage account are taxed in the year they are earned. Interest and non-qualified dividends are taxed at ordinary income tax rates, while qualified dividends and long-term capital gains benefit from lower, preferential capital gains rates. Understanding what belongs in each type of account is essential, as it influences not only your tax obligations but also how much money you'll have available in the short term versus what you'll accumulate for retirement.

Here's some classic Warren Buffett wisdom: **invest in what you know.**[18] Understanding what you're investing in, especially if it aligns with your interests, can help you make more informed decisions and feel more connected to your investments. Plus, supporting industries or areas that excite you is always more engaging.

For instance, I'm particularly interested in technology and AI, as well as travel, e-commerce, and web-based businesses. I also enjoy keeping up with news and politics to anticipate how certain events might influence industries, occasionally investing in temporarily

---

[18] Brian Dolan. Investopedia. July 30, 2024. "Investing Rules the Legendary Warren Buffett Lives By" https://www.investopedia.com/financial-edge/0210/rules-that-warren-buffett-lives-by.aspx

underperforming areas. While this approach involves a higher level of risk, it works for me. That said, it's equally valid — and often wise — to invest in diversified funds that include companies and sectors in which you may not be an expert. Diversification is a key strategy for managing risk, as it helps cushion the impact of market volatility or fluctuations in individual businesses over the long term.

If you're a young adult you've likely heard that younger investors are often advised to allocate a significant portion of their portfolio to aggressive stocks. Why? Because at this stage in life, you have the advantage of time to weather market volatility and capitalize on the potential for long-term growth. That said, it's also wise to set aside a portion of your investments in more conservative options, such as high-grade or government-backed bonds, preferred stocks, or blue-chip companies. These investments may grow more slowly, but they provide stability and help balance the risk in your portfolio.

Why focus on aggressive stocks? Historically, the stock market has outpaced inflation over the long term, and aggressive stocks often deliver higher returns. This methodology means that, over time, they preserve your purchasing power and generate significant capital gains. However, it's important to remember that past performance doesn't guarantee future results, and diversification is key to managing risk.

Apple

Let's look at an example. Imagine you were nineteen in the mid-2000s. Around that time, Steve Jobs had just announced the iPhone, and Apple (AAPL) was gaining attention.[19] You might have thought it was the perfect time to invest in Apple, planning to sell "when it's high." Or, you might have assumed it was too late, believing the opportunity had already passed. Both assumptions could be flawed.

- In January 2006, Apple's stock traded at roughly $2.70 per share (adjusted for splits).
- When the iPhone launched in 2007, the stock was around $3.00.
- By December of that same year, it had climbed to approximately $7.00.

[19] Steven Levy and Karl Montevirgen. Britannica Money. August 7, 2025. "Apple Inc." https://www.britannica.com/money/Apple-Inc

If you sold at $7.00, you might have felt smart for dodging the 2008 financial crisis dip. But from a long-term perspective, you'd have missed out on Apple's continued growth. Over the next decade, the stock rose to $20, then $24, and eventually surpassed $170. The lesson? If your investment philosophy is long-term, don't underestimate the potential of a strong company.[20]

NVIDIA

NVIDIA offers another example. It's a company that has been around for years and is known for its volatility. But consider this: where was NVIDIA 10 years ago, and where might it be 10 or 20 years from now? These are the kinds of questions to ask yourself when you're young and can afford to take on some risk.

If you prefer a more conservative approach, that's perfectly fine. What matters most is aligning your investments with your personal comfort level and financial goals. Options like Treasury bills, bonds, preferred stocks (which often pay dividends), or shares in well-established companies can provide more stability. While these investments may not deliver the dramatic returns of aggressive stocks, they can still grow your wealth over time in a more predictable manner.

As you progress through life, your investment strategy typically becomes more conservative with age. This shift happens gradually as priorities and risk tolerance evolve. That said, there are exceptions. For example, we have clients in their sixties who still invest aggressively — simply because they enjoy it. If they're comfortable with the risks and it brings them genuine satisfaction, we believe that's what truly matters.

Determine how much to invest.

Ultimately, how much you invest is entirely up to you. It depends on factors such as your income, how consistently you save, and how well you manage your spending and emergency fund. For example, let's say you worked a summer job for five years and now have $26,000 left over after fully funding your emergency savings. A solid, baseline aggressive portfolio might look something like this:

---

[20] Yahoo!Finance. 2025. Apple Inc. (AAPL).
https://finance.yahoo.com/quote/AAPL/history/

- **40–50 percent in an ETF or a diversified basket of aggressive stocks.** Providers like Charles Schwab, Fidelity, Vanguard, BlackRock, and WisdomTree offer reputable ETFs. Focus on funds in strong, growing industries likely to remain in demand over time.
- **15–20 percent in international markets.** Diversifying beyond the U.S. allows you to tap into global opportunities, including emerging economies. Look for broad-based international index funds to spread your risk.
- **10 percent in emerging economies.** Think of this as a "growth kicker." While it carries higher volatility, it can offer significant upside potential over the long term.
- **10 percent in bonds.** Bonds act as a cushion, providing stability and protection if the stock market takes a downturn.
- **10–25 percent for "whatever you want."** This approach could be an investment in a small business, a sector you're passionate about, or even something more speculative. Use this portion to learn, experiment, and have fun.

For someone around my age, this breakdown offers a solid starting point. However, it's essential to adapt it to your personal goals, risk tolerance, and any major life events on the horizon. Always keep your emergency fund intact — typically three to six months' worth of living expenses — and consider consulting a financial professional for personalized advice. It can make a big difference in helping you build a strategy that works for you.

Your Financial Journey

You own your financial journey, but you can always map it out and guide it with a helping hand. Find what works best for you. The most important thing is to start early, stay informed, and remain consistent. Over time, you'll thank yourself.

I've done some research for you and put together a few simple allocation examples to give you different starting points based on various perspectives and risk tolerances. I've also thrown in some existing securities as examples to help illustrate your options.

Very Aggressive Portfolio

Objective: Maximize growth by investing heavily in equities across various sectors and regions, with minimal bond allocation for slight stability.

Allocation (100 percent total):

- **50 percent U.S. Large-Cap Growth (Stocks or ETFs)**: Examples: Individual stocks like Apple (AAPL), Microsoft (MSFT), ETFs like Vanguard Growth ETF (VUG) or Invesco QQQ (QQQ)
- **20 percent International & Emerging Markets (ETFs or MFs)**: Examples: iShares Core MSCI Emerging Markets ETF (IEMG), Vanguard Total International Stock Index Fund (VXUS)
- **10 percent Small-Cap Stocks (Stocks or ETFs)**: Examples: iShares Russell 2000 ETF (IWM), Vanguard Small-Cap Growth ETF (VBK)
- **10 percent Sector-Specific/High-Conviction (Stocks, ETFs, or MFs)**: Examples: Technology Select Sector SPDR Fund (XLK), ARK Innovation ETF (ARKK), iShares Global Clean Energy ETF (ICLN), Health Care Select Sector SPDR Fund (XLV)
- **10 percent Bonds or Bond ETFs for Slight Stability**: Examples: Vanguard Total Bond Market ETF (BND), iShares Core U.S. Aggregate Bond ETF (AGG)

Who's it for? Young investors with a high tolerance for market swings who can invest for the long term (10-plus years).

Moderate Portfolio

Objective: Achieve balanced growth and moderate volatility by combining equities with a more substantial bond component.

Allocation (100 percent total):

- **40 percent U.S. Large-Cap Core (Stocks or ETFs)**: Examples: Vanguard Total Stock Market ETF (VTI), Fidelity 500 Index Fund (FXAIX)

- **15 percent International Equity (ETFs or MFs)**: Examples: Vanguard FTSE Developed Markets ETF (VEA), Fidelity Total International Index Fund (FTIHX)
- **10 percent Small/Mid-Cap (Stocks or ETFs)**: Examples: SPDR S&P MidCap 400 ETF (MDY), Vanguard Small-Cap Value ETF (VBR)
- **5 percent Specialty Sector / REITs**: Examples: Vanguard Real Estate ETF (VNQ), Schwab U.S. REIT ETF (SCHH)
- **25 percent Bonds (Mix of Intermediate-Term & High-Quality)**: Examples: Fidelity U.S. Bond Index Fund (FXNAX), Vanguard Intermediate-Term Bond ETF (BIV)
- **5 percent Cash/Cash Equivalents or Short-Term Treasuries**: Examples: High-yield savings account, iShares Short Treasury Bond ETF (SHV)

Who's it for? Investors seeking a balance between growth and stability with medium risk tolerance.

Conservative Portfolio

Objective: Preserve capital and generate steady returns with more emphasis on bonds, while still allowing for some equity growth.

Allocation (100 percent total):
- **30 percent U.S. Large-Cap Blue-Chip Stocks or ETFs**: Examples: Vanguard Dividend Appreciation ETF (VIG), SPDR S&P 500 ETF (SPY)
- **10 percent International Equity (ETFs or MFs)**: Examples: Vanguard Total International Stock ETF (VXUS), iShares Core MSCI EAFE ETF (IEFA)
- **10 percent REITs or Dividend-Focused Funds**: Examples: T. Rowe Price Real Estate (TRREX), ProShares S&P 500 Dividend Aristocrats ETF (NOBL)
- **40 percent Bonds (High-Quality, Investment-Grade)**: Examples: Vanguard Total Bond Market ETF (BND), iShares Core U.S. Aggregate Bond ETF (AGG)
- **10 percent Short-Term Treasuries/High-Yield Savings**: Examples: iShares Short Treasury Bond ETF (SHV), Vanguard Short-Term Corporate Bond ETF (VCSH)

Who's it for? Investors prioritizing capital preservation but still wanting some exposure to equity returns.

Very Conservative Portfolio

Objective: Minimize risk, preserve capital, and generate modest returns. Often suitable for those nearing major financial goals or with low risk tolerance.

Allocation (100 percent total):

- **20 percent High-Quality Dividend-Paying Stocks or ETFs**: Examples: Blue-chip dividend stocks (e.g., Johnson & Johnson (JNJ), Procter & Gamble (PG), Vanguard High Dividend Yield ETF (VYM)

- **10 percent Short-Term Corporate Bonds**: Examples: Vanguard Short-Term Corporate Bond Index Fund (VCSH)

- **50 percent Government & Investment-Grade Bonds**: Examples: Fidelity Intermediate Treasury Bond Index (FUAMX), Vanguard Long-Term Treasury ETF (VGLT) (if comfortable with duration risk)

- **10 percent TIPS (Treasury Inflation-Protected Securities)**: Examples: iShares TIPS Bond ETF (TIP) (Tips are government bonds that do not pay interest but sell at a discount. This means, for example, you buy a TIPS bond at $9,800 with a par value of $10,000, and at maturity, you'll receive $10,000 with a total profit of $200.)

- **10 percent Cash Equivalents/Money Market**: Examples: High-yield savings account, Money market mutual fund (e.g., Vanguard Prime Money Market Fund (VMRXX)

Who's it for? Individuals with a very low appetite for risk — such as those approaching a big purchase, retirees needing capital preservation, or anyone preferring minimal volatility.

CHAPTER 13

Crypto

Picture this: it's 2009, and the world's financial system is still on its knees after the 2008 meltdown, banks collapsed, people lost homes, and trust in the system felt about as strong as a house of cards in a hurricane. Out of the digital shadows comes a mysterious figure, or maybe a group, calling themselves Satoshi Nakamoto. With one white paper, they launched the world's first cryptocurrency, Bitcoin.[21]

No banks, no middlemen, just a way for people to send money digitally, directly to each other. Like Venmo without the bank fees or the government snooping around. Satoshi's idea was a truly independent currency, with no central bank printing money out of thin air and no monetary policy that could devalue your savings overnight.

Here's the kicker: to this day, no one knows who Satoshi is. It's the greatest mystery in modern finance. Some think it's one person, others think it's a group of brilliant coders, a team of cyberpunks, or even an AI. Either way, Satoshi dropped the mic and walked off the stage, leaving behind a revolution that would challenge the very fabric of money as we knew it.

Back in 2010, one of the first real-world Bitcoin transactions went down. A guy named Laszlo Hanyecz bought two pizzas for 10,000 BTC.

---

[21] Dave Birnbaum. Forbes. May 9, 2025. "The History Of Bitcoin: Who Invented It And How It Evolved" https://www.forbes.com/sites/digital-assets/article/the-history-of-bitcoin-who-invented-it/

Those pizzas would be worth hundreds of millions today, a fact that's both hilarious and humbling. That's probably the most expensive lunch in history, and a reminder of just how far crypto has come in such a short time.[22]

Let's not stop there, because Bitcoin's story is just the beginning of the cryptocurrency saga. In the years that followed, Bitcoin grew from a digital curiosity for a handful of programmers into a financial phenomenon that would capture the attention of Wall Street, Silicon Valley, and regulators worldwide. At first, it was the domain of hackers and libertarians who wanted a financial system that governments or big banks couldn't control.[23]

Bitcoin mining, the process that keeps the network running, started as a hobby for tech enthusiasts with a decent computer. But as Bitcoin's price rose, the math problems miners had to solve got harder, and the competition grew fiercer.[24] Before long, warehouses full of high-powered computers, called mining farms, arose across China, Iceland, and later the U.S., all vying for the digital gold rush.[25]

Bitcoin's price is primarily driven by supply and demand, but it's also heavily influenced by factors like market sentiment, news, regulations, and technological developments. When people get excited about Bitcoin's potential, prices can skyrocket. When fear hits the market, it can crash like a lead balloon.[26] Just think back to 2017, when Bitcoin's price went from around $1,000 to nearly $20,000 in a single year,

[22] Colin Harper. CoinDesk. May 22, 2025. "What You Didn't Know About Laszlo Hanyecz, the Bitcoin Pizza Day Legend"
https://www.coindesk.com/tech/2025/05/22/what-you-didnt-know-about-laszlo-hanyecz-the-bitcoin-pizza-day-legend
[23] Argo. 2025. "Bitcoin & Institutional Investors | A Shifting Landscape"
https://www.argoblockchain.com/articles/how-institutions-changed-their-mind-on-bitcoin
[24] Gerrit van Sittert. ASIC Jungle. September 24, 2022. "The History and Evolution of Bitcoin Mining" https://asicjungle.com/asic-magazine/articles/the-history-and-evolution-of-bitcoin-mining
[25] Sunbird. 2025. "Largest Bitcoin Mining Farms in the World"
https://www.sunbirddcim.com/sites/default/files/Sunbird_InfoGraphic_Bitcoin.pdf
[26] Andrew Bloomenthal. Investopedia. June 17, 2025. "What Determines Bitcoin's Price?" https://www.investopedia.com/tech/what-determines-value-1-bitcoin/

plummeting to $3,000 the following year.[27] Or in 2021, when it soared to over $60,000, thanks in part to tweets from Elon Musk, before crashing again when China cracked down on mining.[28] That kind of volatility would make even the most seasoned investor's head spin.

The anonymity of Bitcoin's creator adds another layer of intrigue. Some call Satoshi a financial superhero; others see them as a threat to the old guard. Either way, Satoshi's disappearance left a decentralized system that no single person can control. That's the beauty, and the risk, of Bitcoin.

Bitcoin's rise paved the way for thousands of other cryptocurrencies, from Ethereum to Dogecoin to Solana. Some were serious projects aiming to revolutionize finance, while others were jokes that somehow ended up worth billions. Remember Dogecoin? It started as a meme, a way to poke fun at the hype, but after some celebrity tweets and online buzz, it soared like a rocket. Proof that in crypto, even a joke can become a jackpot if enough people believe in it.

How It Works: The Blockchain Beat

So how does all this actually work? At the heart of crypto is the **blockchain**. Think of it as a giant, unchangeable notebook that everyone can see, but no one can fudge the numbers. Every Bitcoin transaction is recorded in that ledger forever, out in the open for all to see. That is why some argue it is so powerful and consider it transparent and secure.

Mining is how new Bitcoins come to life. Picture a global digital gold rush: thousands of supercomputers racing to solve insane math puzzles. The first one to crack the code validates a "block" of transactions and earns some fresh Bitcoin as a reward. It's like a video game where the prize is money, except the competition is fierce and the math is brutal.

---

[27] John Edwards. Investopedia. May 22, 2025. "Bitcoin's Price History" https://www.investopedia.com/articles/forex/121815/bitcoins-price-history.asp

[28] Alexander Reed, Alex Benfield. 99 Bitcoins. June 16, 2025. "Bitcoin Historical Price & Events" https://99bitcoins.com/cryptocurrency/bitcoin/historical-price/

At first, you could mine Bitcoin with a decent laptop. These days? You're going up against massive data centers burning enough electricity to power small countries. That's how big this has gotten.

The Risks: Volatility and the Wild Ride

Here's the deal: crypto is the Wild West of investing. One day, you're on top of the world, watching your portfolio climb like a rocket ship; the next day, you're underwater, wondering where everything went wrong. Bitcoin's price soared from under a dollar to over $60,000, then crashed to $20,000 like a rock skipping across a pond.[29] That kind of volatility makes seasoned investors sweat and thrill-seekers grin.

Just look at Mt. Gox, one of the first big Bitcoin exchanges that started in the early days. It was *the* place to trade crypto, the Wild West's biggest saloon where everyone gathered. Until 2014, when it got hacked, and boom, 850,000 Bitcoins vanished into thin air.[30] That was like billions of dollars, gone overnight, with no safety net, FDIC, or government rescue plan. The financial gut punch taught the crypto world a painful lesson about security and trust.

Or take Terra Luna, a so-called stablecoin that was supposed to hold its value steady like the dollar. Instead, in 2022, it collapsed spectacularly, wiping out $60 billion in market value and taking a lot of investors down with it.[31] People who thought they were playing it safe suddenly found themselves broke, staring at computer screens in disbelief. Terra's meltdown reminded everyone that even "safe" bets can go south in a hurry in crypto.

Then there was FTX, the exchange that promised to be the safe place to trade crypto, the one with celebrity endorsements, fancy logos, and a founder who wore a hoodie and played the role of the "crypto

---

[29] John Edwards. Investopedia. August 15, 2025. "Bitcoin's Price History" https://www.investopedia.com/articles/forex/121815/bitcoins-price-history.asp
[30] Investopedia. April 23, 2024. "What Was Mt. Gox? Definition, History, Collapse, and Future" https://www.investopedia.com/terms/m/mt-gox.asp
[31] MacKenzie Sigalos. CNBC Crypto World. May 28, 2022. "$60 billion collapse of major cryptocurrency is not the industry's Bear Stearns moment – senators and regulators explain why" https://www.cnbc.com/2022/05/28/60-billion-terra-washout-not-cryptos-bear-stearns-moment-regulators.html

genius." Turns out, it was run like a house of cards. When it all fell apart in 2022, billions in customer funds went missing. It was like watching a financial train wreck in slow motion, the kind you can't look away from, even though you know the ending will be ugly.[32]

And let's not forget those tweets from Elon Musk, the guy who's like the puppet master of crypto prices. One minute, he's sending Dogecoin to the moon with a single word, "Doge,"[33] the next, he's tanking Bitcoin with a casual post about "environmental concerns."[34] That's the power of social media in the crypto world, where a single tweet can wipe out billions in market value, leaving traders scrambling to make sense of it all.

That's volatility, plain and simple, and that's what makes crypto exciting, unpredictable, and, let's be honest, dangerous. It's a place where fortunes are made and lost in the blink of an eye, where the thrill of the next big win keeps investors coming back for more, even after the dust from the last crash hasn't even settled.

Imagine being able to send money across the planet instantly, 24/7, without waiting for a bank to open or a wire transfer to clear, no more bank holidays or business hours, no more "sorry, come back Monday" nonsense. That's the promise of crypto, and the best part is, it's already happening. People are sending Bitcoin, Ethereum, and other cryptos across borders, skipping the red tape and the fees, with a few taps on their phone.

Here's my take: crypto might be the future of money, or it might just be a stepping stone to something even bigger. Either way, it's worth understanding. **But don't get swept up in the hype**. Do your research.

---

[32] MacKenzie Sigalos. CNBC. November 12, 2022. "Between $1billion and $2 billion of FTX customer funds have disappeared, SBF had a secret 'back door' to transfer billions: Report" https://www.cnbc.com/2022/11/12/1-billion-to-2-billion-of-ftx-customer-funds-missing-report.html

[33] Chris Isidore. CNN Business. February 4, 2021. "Elon Musk tweeted. Dogecoin surged more than 50%" https://www.cnn.com/2021/02/04/investing/elon-musk-dogecoin

[34] Ryan Browne. CNBC. May 13, 2021. "Why everyone from Elon Musk to Janet Yellen is worried about bitcoin's energy usage" https://www.cnbc.com/2021/05/13/why-elon-musk-is-worried-about-bitcoin-environmental-impact.html

Start small if you choose to explore it. Never invest what you can't afford to lose. Crypto is like a rollercoaster, thrilling, but you need to buckle up and hold on tight.

The bottom line: crypto is a new frontier. And like any frontier, it's full of opportunity and full of risk. The choice is yours: jump in with both feet or watch from the sidelines. But no matter what, don't ignore it.

Crypto is different from traditional investments like stocks or bonds. The U.S. dollar is backed by the full faith and credit of the United States; stocks are backed by the underlying companies and traded on regulated exchanges; and gold is supported by a physical asset. Most cryptocurrencies are not backed by any government, company, or tangible commodity. Their value depends entirely on what buyers and sellers are willing to pay. They are also not insured by the FDIC or SIPC, meaning you could lose your entre investment if the platform or token fails. Crypto carries unique risks that make it important to approach with caution.

CHAPTER 14

Voices of the Masters

Enough of this guy. I want to hear what other people think.

Well, I have great news for you! I did that. I compiled and interviewed some distinguished figures (within their own fields, practices, or industries), and I asked them to "tell me five points of advice for those aged eighteen to twenty-eight, new to the investment, financial, or work-world."

The responses I received were extraordinary.

These are outstanding individuals in my eyes. The voices, philosophies and opinions are so diverse and invaluable. I made a great effort to keep their responses as unfiltered and raw as possible, while also making it appropriate for a book. I have a lot of respect for everyone who participated. You'll be shocked at how simultaneously similar and diverse all the advice is. Take note of them with the attitude to observe, learn, think and (most importantly) respect.

To all who contributed, **thank you** for helping my generation!

Mike Meek, M.B. Meek Group

1. **"Avoid unnecessary debt.** Live within your means to avoid the common trap of spending money as soon as you earn it. Prioritize saving overspending on depreciating assets that do not contribute to wealth accumulation."

2. **"Invest regularly.** Commit a portion of every paycheck, such as 10 percent, to investments that can grow over time, such as stocks or mutual funds. Treat this money as if it's already gone, focusing on its future value rather than its immediate absence from your budget."

3. **"Be okay with not knowing.** Always be willing to admit when you don't know something and commit to finding the answer."

4. **"Embrace your age as an advantage.** Don't let your age be a barrier. Confidence and the ability to engage intelligently in investments, conversations, or anything can make age irrelevant. This is particularly important for young professionals who may feel intimidated in areas 'dominated' by older people."

5. **"Fake it till you make it with integrity.** Use strategic questioning to navigate areas where your knowledge may be limited. This doesn't mean being deceitful but rather being clever about guiding conversations to learn and adapt quickly. Always be willing to admit when you don't know something and commit to finding the answer."

A closer look at Mike Meek

Mike Meek is the pure essence of an entrepreneur. He launched his first venture straight out of high school, running his own hay crew, and has never looked back. Over the decades he founded and led multiple companies, advised more than 30,000 leaders worldwide, and built a reputation as a master of firm management, leadership development, and strategic execution. As founder of M.B. Meek Group, he provides outsourced CEO and organizational strategy services, helping companies scale and restructure leadership teams so they can thrive without bottlenecks.

Beyond the impressive résumé — Hall of Fame collegiate athlete, keynote speaker to governments and global firms, PhD candidate in

Organizational Leadership — what sets Mike apart is his humility, gratitude, and relentless work ethic. He lives what he teaches, combining sharp business acumen with interpersonal genius. Whether guiding a boardroom or coaching youth athletics, Mike blends integrity with a gift for empowering others, making him one of the most grounded and inspiring business leaders you could hope to meet.

Poppy, Schroer Implement Company, Schroer Farms

1. "**Start planning** what you want your life to look like at sixty. Focus on acquiring a good education and setting achievable three to five-year goals to keep your life on track."
2. "**Live at home** as long as you can to save money, invest in your education, get good at time management, and develop strong work habits. Also, consider taking courses that relate to your career to enhance your skills and make you more credible."
3. "**Join a group** like a men's dinner club that meets once a week. These groups give you networks, friendship, and support."
4. "**Make sure you have someone** you can trust to talk to when you are upset."
5. "**Don't drink too much.**"
6. "**Bonus Point:** Be a good listener."

A closer look at "Poppy" (Walter Schroer)

Walter "Poppy" Schroer is a lifelong entrepreneur whose career has spanned farming, agribusiness, and industrial-scale operations. Known for his stoicism, discipline, and unwavering work ethic, he built and ran several successful ventures, including an industrial chicken-hatchery farm, before retiring in his mid-eighties.

To his family, Poppy is more than an accomplished businessman — he is a mentor and example of what it means to live with integrity. Now enjoying retirement in southern Georgia, he remains a steady, guiding presence whose wisdom reflects decades of perseverance and quiet leadership.

Rob Townsend, The British Voiceover

1. "My first piece of advice is **not to waste time during your school years.** I did this and had to redouble my efforts to catch up, but in fairness, that was the nature of the public education system back then."

2. "**Try and save.** I would try and do this as a boy and young teenager, but when I began working at Angell, I was able to do this more consistently. I was not earning good money initially. In fact, my first salary from them was £4,500 a year. But, by saving regularly, within three years, I had enough money for a deposit for my first apartment."

3. "**When money is tight,** for goodness' sake, don't waste money by increasing your debt, in order to rip out a perfectly good bathroom or kitchen, perhaps old, to replace it with a new one. I never did this and benefited accordingly. I would also say buy clothes when they're on sale. I still do this. Also buy discounted food, if you can. For example, food that is beyond date can sometimes be had for 50 per cent off. These kinds of savings, as well as preparing food at home, can enable more to be put into savings accounts."

4. "**If you happen to have a mortgage, pay off more than you need to.** You then keep ahead of any rises in interest rates and if rates happen to fall, keep that extra payment going as you will reduce your capital."

5. "**Don't forget to save.** Save money in a high interest account so you can use that balance to pay off your mortgage. I was able to pay into this kind of account, simply by being cautious. For example, bringing my own sandwiches to work saved me a fortune. Not going out to eat regularly and if you really want to push this, which I did, don't go on trips you can ill afford, rather, pay off the mortgage."

6. "**Do as much as you can to pay off any mortgage** as soon as you can. Just because you have a twenty-five year term, doesn't mean you have to keep it for that long. I never got any big financial help from my family as that kind of money wasn't around. My mum passed with £1,200 to her name and no

property. I completed my mortgage in nine years. I had sold my apartment and bought a small house, the one I live in today. Yes, it is tiny but that is the nature of property over here [in London]. Paying off my mortgage enabled me to save and buy another property just around the corner from this one and also my property in Canada. It also meant I was able to save more than most. This has enabled me to pay for Dominic's [Rob's son] university fees and also pay for the fees of Lena's children [the children from his recently married wife]."

A closer look at Rob Townsend

Rob Townsend is a London-based sound engineer and professional voice actor known for his distinctive style as "The British Voiceover." His career began in the heart of the U.K.'s legendary audio scene, including a tenure at Angel Recording Studios near Abbey Road, where he worked alongside some of the industry's most talented engineers.

Today, Rob operates his own practice, lending his voice and production skills to video games, commercials, documentaries, and corporate projects worldwide. His work on *Safe Money Strategies* as producer has also made him a familiar voice to Kelly Financial clients. With his humor, craftsmanship, and generosity, Rob is both a consummate professional and a friend whose voice has carried across continents.

Mark O'ffill, ABO Solution

1. **"Save and invest."**
2. **"Your word and your reputation** are the most important and most valuable assets you have."
3. **"Balance your life."** Every day will be different, but over the long term, make work, sleep, contemplative, and expressive time equally important."
4. **"Quality** is more important than quantity."
5. "You can't give anything to anyone more valuable than your **time.**"
6. "Bonus: Do unto others as they'd **like done unto them.** (the Platinum rule)"

More advice from Mark O'ffill:

7. **"Give value** and expect the same from others."
8. **"Coach/Teach."**
9. **"Listen** more than you speak."
10. "Know, or learn, the difference between **criticism and critique.**"
11. **"Be chivalrous.** Hold a lady's chair, open her door, and cover her shoulders when it is cold."

From my correspondence with Mark:

12. "Your original question included 'and exploring investing' so, **invest in what you know.**"
13. "Warren Buffett is a billionaire because he was patient, he studied, and he learned. **He didn't chase fads.**"
14. "Mark Zuckerberg is a billionaire because **he 'started' a fad.**"

A closer look at Mark O'ffill

Mark O'ffill is CEO of Advisors Back Office Solution (ABO Solution) and a founding partner of Prairie Fire Resources, LLC. A CPA and U.S. Navy veteran, Mark's career spans more than three decades of accounting, tax strategy, and financial consulting. He has also been active in venture capital and business operations, with a particular gift for building and refining systems that help organizations scale effectively.

Known for his thoughtful, philosophical approach to business and life, Mark is both a rigorous thinker and a generous mentor. Whether working through complex tax strategy, fine-tuning an Excel model, or exploring the deeper "why" behind a decision, he brings clarity and creativity in equal measure. Above all, Mark is a loyal friend and confidant, deeply committed to helping others succeed.

Dr. Grace Vuoto, *The Conversation with Stephen & Grace*

1. "**Number one is to live according to the faith** that we hold dear, which is [their] faith of the Catholic Church not just outwardly, but authentically, and to uphold those virtues. From that, I believe every good thing flows. **Put God above all things.**"

2. "**One of the most important decisions you make** quite early in life is whom you're going to marry. You really have to have a pure heart and look for the right things. When you make that choice well, so much of your life falls into place, and you avoid terrible heartaches or causing pain to your children."

3. "**When deciding your profession, we always advise: follow your passion.** Don't think, 'How am I gonna make money?' because if you're just pursuing money and it's something you don't like, you'll be miserable and won't succeed. On the other hand, if it's something you love — even if people say it's not lucrative — you're going to do extremely well because you have the passion, and that will be rewarded."

4. "**Do not, under any circumstances, get into debt.** You'll be tempted to keep up with the Jones, to have a flashy car or a bigger house than you can afford, but that causes tremendous pressure on you, your household, and your marriage. As soon as you can, pay off your primary residence. Get a reasonable house, and pay it off as quickly as you can, because then you're not stuck with a huge mortgage and can invest that money in other projects."

5. "**Give everybody as big a chance as you possibly can.** Have a generous, big, bountiful heart, forgive generously, and only draw the line if someone commits a grave wrong against you or causes serious harm. I've seen people cut others off for small slights, especially family members, but I believe we should connect on their virtue and overlook friction. That makes everyone happier and sets a great example for your children. It also creates a richer life with a wide variety of people in your circle."

A closer look at Dr. Grace Vuoto

Dr. Grace Vuoto is a political analyst, writer, and broadcaster whose career spans academia and media. She has served as an editorial writer and columnist for *The Washington Times* and has co-hosted the weekly radio show *The Conversation with Stephen and Grace* on WXTK 95.1 FM, where she provided cultural and political commentary to a wide New England audience.

With a PhD and decades of teaching and writing experience, Dr. Vuoto brings intellectual rigor to public discourse. Yet what makes her distinctive is her generosity of spirit, her faith, and her ability to connect with listeners on deeply human issues. Her voice has guided audiences not just toward political understanding, but toward richer, more meaningful lives.

Jeff Kuhner, *The Kuhner Report*

1. **"Choose work you love**. Outside of picking your husband or your wife — because that is the most important decision you make — I always told my students [when he was a professor at McGill]: the best advice you can ever get about your career or economic future is this: you're not going to spend more time on anything else in your life than at work. If you're fortunate to have a good job, that's where you'll be most of your day, five days a week, sometimes more. So you have to love your job. If you're just doing something for money or to please others, you'll be unhappy, and by your thirties or forties, you'll have a big career midlife crisis anyway. But if you pursue what you truly love — even if the salary isn't as high at first — every day you wake up happy, you go to work happy, you're fulfilled. That's the ultimate victory. You're going to enjoy life and ultimately be successful."

2. **"Take pride in your work**. Number two to me is the only way to live. It's not just finances or employment — do everything to the best of your abilities. If you're flipping hamburgers, do it well. Don't be sloppy. Don't rush. There's such tremendous satisfaction from doing a job well. I'm in a competitive business, talk radio, but to me what's important is that you tried your best. If you gave it everything you have, that's all you can do. Always do your work with pride, effort, and excellence."

3. **"Avoid unmanageable debt**. When it comes to budgeting and financing, take this to the bank: avoid debt at all costs. This is the biggest cause of unhappiness, misery, and even relationship failures. It's a marriage killer. If you're constantly behind on payments, always short of money, and feeding interest on debt, it creates never-ending stress. People buy houses or cars they can't afford, put vacations on credit cards at 20 percent, and soon they're drowning. Better to get a smaller home or a more modest car — manageable debt. Over time, as you handle finances responsibly, you can buy the house or car of your dreams. But don't sink yourself into massive debt. It destroys marriages, wrecks relationships, and can lead to heart attacks, strokes, and depression. Live within your means."

4. **"When you see 'radical' rhetoric, do the opposite.** I learned this at sixteen, and it has guided me in my career, finances, life, marriage, everything: whatever radical ideologies say, do the opposite. I'm serious. I've seen the radicalism mantra. 'Divorce is liberating,' 'Have multiple partners,' 'Drugs will expand your consciousness,' and it almost always ends in disaster. A lot of this advice goes against fundamental principles tied to human nature and God's natural law. If you just do the opposite of what they're pushing, you're going to have a happy, successful life."

5. **"Honor God, Country, and Family.** There are fundamental, eternal principles that transcend everything: God, country, and family.

    a. **Family**: Nothing satisfies you more than having a family, wife, husband, children, grandchildren, uncles, grandparents. It's the purpose and meaning of life.

    b. **Country**: Appreciate everything this country has to offer: its freedoms, opportunities, and liberties.

    c. Recognize our life was given to us by **God**, Almighty, and serve His will. If you do these three things, you will succeed in business, work, finance, relationships — and above all, in life."

A closer look at Jeff Kuhner

Jeffrey T. Kuhner is the host of *The Kuhner Report* on WRKO-AM 680 in Boston, one of New England's most popular talk radio programs. A political commentator and journalist, he previously served as editor of *Insight on the News* and has written for national publications including *The Washington Times*. His sharp analysis and unapologetic style have made him a well-known figure in conservative media.

Beyond broadcasting, Jeff is admired by his listeners for his passion and conviction. He speaks not only about politics but also about values — faith, family, and country — that shape the lives of his audience. His ability to blend intellectual commentary with heartfelt conviction has earned him both respect and loyalty from his community of listeners.

John Budris, *Safe Money Strategies* (Radio Show)

1. **"Make sure you understand what 'investing' means.** Investing doesn't only mean the purchase of some financial instrument in the present for the purposes of selling at a profit later in the future. An investment in experience at a young age is often as valuable — if not more valuable. For instance, traveling or taking specialized courses not only broadens your horizons but can open doors to new opportunities and enrich your personal and professional life significantly."

2. **"People in their twenties have a long life ahead, but the golden years will arrive faster than they can imagine.** What seems like a small amount invested into something each month builds up to a significant nest egg later. Consistently saving a portion of your income, even if it seems small, leverages the power of compounding interest over decades, turning modest savings into substantial retirement funds."

3. **"Cultivate hobbies** that you not only enjoy but that can accumulate value over time. Becoming knowledgeable in areas like rare coins, unusual firearms, antiques, or artwork can bring enormous pleasure and financial benefits. Savvy collectors can have fun while they build equity in their collections. For example, when I was a schoolteacher and financially constrained, I bought an old Martin guitar for $500 at a pawn shop. The pleasure it has brought me over four decades is immeasurable, and its value now is north of $5,000."

4. **"The best bits of wisdom will always come from those who have lived through challenging times,** like my father, a child of The Great Depression. Their experiences teach us the value of saving, the importance of frugality, and the benefits of a long-term perspective in both financial planning and personal investment."

5. **"Starting your investment journey early is crucial.** It's not just about how much you invest, but how soon you start. Early investments in the financial markets or in personal growth can grow exponentially due to the additional time they have to appreciate in value."

A closer look at John Budris

John Budris is a journalist, editor, and broadcaster whose career spans print and radio. He is co-host of *Safe Money Strategies*™ alongside the Kelly Financial team, where his background in storytelling and news analysis brings clarity and depth to financial discussions.

John has held senior editorial roles in New England media and served as editor of *Vineyard Style Magazine*, where he shaped narratives that connected culture, community, and personal finance. With his sharp wit, broad knowledge, and gift for connecting dots across fields, John continues to be both an insightful commentator and an engaging communicator.

Lloyd Granoff, Granoff Associates

1. **"Don't just follow the path others have set out for you.** As a young person, it's okay to explore less certain roads. This can be an exciting way to discover what truly fulfills you in life."

2. **"Remember, life is about taking chances.** Sometimes, venturing into the unknown can lead you to the most rewarding experiences. Don't be afraid to step off the beaten track to pursue what really interests you."

3. **"At many points in life, you'll come to a fork in the road.** Once you make a decision, focus on moving forward rather than second-guessing your choices. Looking back might distract you from making the most of your current path."

4. **"When it comes to investing,** my top tip is to cut your losses early. If an investment is losing money, it's wise to sell it quickly to prevent a small loss from becoming a much larger one."

5. **"On the flip side, when you have investments that are performing well,** let them continue to grow. It's generally beneficial to hold on to successful positions and only sell small portions if necessary. This approach allows you to maximize potential gains."

A closer look at Lloyd Granoff

Lloyd W. Granoff is a seasoned real estate developer and private equity investor, serving as managing member of Granoff Associates, LLC. For nearly three decades he has overseen commercial, residential, and mixed-use property development, with prior leadership roles at Wallace Capital Corporation and Secure Records Management.

A Boston College graduate, Lloyd combines financial acumen with a deep commitment to strategic growth and due diligence. He is also active in philanthropic and civic endeavors, reflecting a lifelong dedication to community building alongside business success.

David Callanan, Advisors Excel

1. **"I only asked my daughters to read a couple of books.** One is *Soundtracks* by Jon Acuff. We often tell ourselves stories that aren't true. We need to be intentional about the stories we do tell ourselves because mindset matters a lot!"

2. **"I dislike when people tell young people to avoid social media** because that's just old people not understanding it. However, understand that what you post is a public document that others will often use to find faults and gaps. Use social media wisely."

3. **"This is specific to our family** — if you make a mistake, know that we will not condone the mistake, but we will always support and love you. So, never fear bringing us into a problem. We can and will help."

4. **"We are always your biggest cheerleaders**, key coaches, and a shoulder to comfort. I've also talked to my daughters about knowing your cheerleaders outside of Mom and Dad, having coaches outside of Mom and Dad, and having friends you can be authentic with."

5. **"Set big goals and, differing from the books**, don't worry about how long they take. The journey to excellence and accomplishment is fun — don't let a time restraint discourage you, instead rely on diligence."

6. **"Know how you learn best and do it consistently.** I love to read; you may not but find out how you learn best. Identify specific strengths you want to enhance and invest time learning from the best."

7. **"Most life-long friendships happen after the age of eighteen, in my experience.** You might have a hundred acquaintances but be discerning about your best five friends — they will impact you significantly. I didn't do this back in the day, but creating a short list of five things they won't be and five things they will might be helpful."

8. **"This advice I give to my girls: boys require respect."**

9. **"Things aren't that cool, in my opinion.** A few things might be but not many and not a lot. Almost all experiences are cool — invest in experiences. Consider creating a bucket list."

Later during a phone conversation with Dave in the airport,

10. **"You need to create a constraint on how much you're going to spend.** A lot of books say 20 percent or 10 percent. I say pick a fixed dollar amount you put into savings every paycheck, like $100 every two weeks. If you don't see it, you won't spend it. You can always live on a little less if you never see that money in the first place."

11. **"Credit cards kill young people.** The interest can eat you alive, and they make it easy to lose track of what you're spending. You scan the card and don't realize how much has gone out. If you have savings set aside, you won't get trapped by credit card debt when emergencies happen. Otherwise, you'll pile it on, and it can wreck your finances long-term."

12. **"Young people should get engaged with investing as soon as possible.** You're good at processing information, so develop a plan you're excited about. Over the long term, equity markets will give you a superior opportunity if you're patient. I coach my kids: 70–80 percent in good ETFs for a foundation, then 20–30 percent in stocks or companies they find interesting. My daughters bought Apple and Google, and one even bought Build-A-Bear, which I thought was crazy, but it soared. The point is, if you're interested, you'll follow it more closely and learn."

13. **"If your job offers a 401(k) and a match, always contribute at least up to the match.** It's essentially free money, like a guaranteed 100 percent return. Young people sometimes say they don't have the money to contribute, but you have to figure it out. You're better off constraining yourself now than missing free money and hurting your long-term savings."

14. **"Living with discipline as a single person is easier than trying to learn it when you have a spouse and kids.** If you can bring good financial habits into a marriage, you're bringing real value. I see so many marriages stressed or broken by debt.

Living beyond your means and accumulating credit card debt creates huge problems that spill into all areas of life."

A closer look at David Callanan

David Callanan is the co-founder of Advisors Excel, one of the most influential independent marketing organizations for financial advisors in the United States. Since 2005, he has helped build AE into a national leader in practice management, marketing, and advisor support, working with thousands of professionals across the country. A graduate of Washburn University, Dave combines sharp business instincts with a rare ability to see opportunities where others see obstacles.

But beyond the numbers, Dave is known for his generosity and heart. He invests deeply in his family and community, modeling the same values he encourages in his advisors. He is a mentor, a coach, and a cheerleader — not just to his daughters, but to countless professionals who have grown under his guidance. His energy is contagious, his belief in people unwavering, and his willingness to share both wisdom and encouragement makes him a leader people genuinely want to follow.

Bob and Rose Grace, Grace Advisory Group

1. "Take 10 or 15 percent of your check and put it in a safe investment."
2. "Don't spend more than you make."
3. "Put money in a Roth IRA."
4. "Always do what is right and honest."
5. "Follow your principles and show respect to your elders."

A closer look at Bob and Rose Grace

Robert E. "Bob" Grace, JD, CLU, ChFC, is president and founder of Grace Advisory Group in Florida, a retirement-focused firm that integrates financial planning, tax strategy, and estate law. He is also an accomplished author, radio host, and frequent public speaker, known for helping retirees build security and confidence in their financial futures. His practice has been recognized repeatedly as one of Southwest Florida's leading advisory firms.

Alongside Bob is his wife, Rose, who has been central to the Grace family's life and legacy. Beyond their professional accomplishments, Bob and Rose have been family friends of the Kellys for over a decade. To those who know them, they represent generosity, warmth, and principle — the kind of people whose character is as rich as their professional success.

Coach Mike McLarney, McLaughlin Research Corporation

1. "**Master your mind.** Build self-awareness, focus deeply, and train your attention like a muscle."

2. "**Embrace lifelong learning!** Read widely, ask better questions, and treat every experience as training."

3. "**Manage stress on purpose.** Notice early signals, respond calmly, and balance effort with real recovery."

4. "**Strengthen your body every day.** Move, fuel well, sleep like a pro, and hydrate."

5. "**Clarify your values and live by them.** Resilience grows when purpose is non-negotiable."

6. "**Define success for yourself.** Set goals that fit your gifts, measure what matters, and adapt as you grow."

7. "**Build deep relationships.** Listen with empathy, communicate honestly, and invest in other people."

8. "**Choose your circle wisely.** The right teammates will challenge you and lift you higher."

9. "**Take bold action now.** Start before you feel ready, learn by doing, and stay consistent."

10. "**Celebrate wins, big and small.** Discipline plus gratitude sustains momentum."

A closer look at Mike McLarney

Michael ("Mike") McLarney is an acquisitions engineer at McLaughlin Research Corporation in Newport, RI, where he supports Navy programs across engineering, logistics, program, and financial management. A Navy-trained Lean Six Sigma Black Belt, he's spent more than two decades leading complex construction, commissioning, and facilities projects — previously serving as senior project manager at URS (AECOM) and senior commissioning authority at WorkingBuildings, with earlier roles managing large metals-processing installations at Danieli Corporation. He holds both a B.S. in Marine Engineering and an M.S. in Facilities Management from Massachusetts Maritime Academy.

Beyond the résumé, Coach Mike is the definition of "get in there and fix it" — a builder of systems, teams, and people. On the mat and in life, he teaches scope control, clarity under pressure, and competitive joy: define the problem, do the work, and win with integrity while lifting others along the way. He is also a Hall of Fame wrestler, **and one hell of a coach.**

Joe DeSimone, State Street Bank

1. "**Always respect your parents.** Your parents only want the best for you. God commands us to honor them."

2. "**Ignore the lunatics.** You will meet some people in life who aren't of the highest caliber. Ignore them. Focus on the good people in your life, God, and your relationship with Him."

3. "**Eat well.** The world is full of junk food. Even the 'organic' food we eat has bad stuff in it. Only treat your body with good stuff — and you will feel much better."

4. "**Dress sharp.** What you wear, and how you appear, is a reflection of who you are. It is something you can control, which is why it's important to do it right."

5. "**Love God.** He has given you the gift of life, family, opportunity, and His eternal kingdom."

6. "**America has a place for you.** If you live in the United States, you live in the greatest country in the world. You have fundamental freedoms, economic prosperity, and the chance at a great life. Work hard for it."

A closer look at Joe DeSimone

Joe DeSimone is one of our family's dearest friends, and the man who gave me my very first haircut at just three years of age — a craft he learned from his father. He and his family immigrated to the United States from Italy as first-generation Italians, escaping Benito Mussolini's fascist regime in the 1940s. Few people better embody both the richness of Italian heritage and the promise of the American dream. Joe deeply appreciates the gift and relief that America provides to those in search of freedom and prosperity.

He is, in every sense, the most authentically Italian man I know — devoted to God, family, and country, in that order. Joe is a true gentleman of culture, with a refined sense of personal fashion, a love of Italian cuisine, and an unmatched skill in barbering. Professionally, he spent more than thirty years working in the computer department at State Street, where he built a long and respected career before retiring. Today, he enjoys life in downtown Boston alongside his incredible sister, Lucia. Joe DeSimone stands as a beaming example of the American immigrant story: faithful, hardworking, and proud of both his heritage and the life he built in this country.

Heidi Cox, Valdosta State University

1. **"The number one most important relationship** is having a personal relationship with Jesus Christ as your Lord and Savior!"
2. **"Accomplishments are noteworthy,** but true success is following and completing the true purpose
3. **"Integrity** is your arsenal!"
4. **"Time is on your side!** Start investing early, even if it's just mutual funds or solid growth stocks that pay dividends for reinvesting!"
5. **"Diversify, diversify, diversify!"**

A closer look a Heidi

Heidi Cox, my amazing aunt, is the Chief Audit Officer of Internal Audit at Valdosta State University, where she leads with over two decades of experience in both public and private accounting. Her career spans roles as a financial advisor, external auditor, and more than fourteen years dedicated to internal auditing within the University System of Georgia. Heidi is licensed as a Certified Public Accountant (CPA) and is also a Certified Internal Auditor (CIA).

Heidi Cox exemplifies the highest standards of the auditing profession while giving back to both her university and the broader accounting community. Essentially, nothing gets past her, so don't mess with her! She is primarily a devoted Christian, wife, and mother of two sons, who make her proud every single day.

Voices of Kelly Financial Services

K elly Financial Services features professionals from diverse backgrounds, walks of life, experiences, and education. They are professionals at their craft and, to their core, care about the client — their livelihood and investments. Kelly Financial Services has been a staple in the greater Boston community for over twenty years and has earned its reputation.

I am proud to call Kelly Financial Services my family business, and these next pieces of contribution are a culmination of what the team has to say to you, the reader. I personally hold each individual on this page in high regard and have great respect for them. I am proud to know and work with them. I believe they each deserve their own unique chapter, as they play a distinct role in the financial world and industry, with a fiduciary duty to help others.

Greg Murray, Kelly Financial Services

1. **"Educate yourself.** Enhance your knowledge to make well-informed decisions. If your income is $30,000, consider opening a Roth IRA due to your lower tax bracket. If you earn $50,000, a traditional IRA might be beneficial because it offers a tax deduction."

2. **"Maximize company benefits.** Utilize every benefit your employer offers. For example, Lowe's provides a 401(k), stock purchase plans, and the option to buy company stock at a discounted rate. Seize these opportunities to enhance your financial portfolio."

3. **"Make sure you have an Exit Strategy.** When investing in individual stocks, it's crucial to have an exit strategy. For instance, during the GameStop surge, many rode the wave up, but then also rode the wave down. If you invest $500 and it grows to $1,000, consider selling half to recover your initial investment. That way, any remaining investment increase is a profit, but if it goes down, even to zero, you technically never lost anything."

4. **"Invest as much as you can without sacrificing your current standard of living.** This strategy helps build a secure financial future without sacrificing your present needs."

5. **"Seek a financial advisor when needed.** If you feel unsure or overwhelmed by the investment world, don't hesitate to consult a financial professional. They can provide guidance and ensure that your investments are managed wisely and are aligned with your financial goals."

A closer look at Greg Murray

Greg Murray is senior vice president and chief compliance officer at Kelly Financial Services, where he has been an anchor of the firm for more than fifteen years. In addition to his compliance leadership, Greg has served as the unofficial chief technology officer and continues to advise clients as a registered investment advisor representative. His professional path reflects both sharp technical instincts and a rare ability to think outside the box, blending financial strategy with a strong grasp of emerging technologies.

Greg is also known for his global outlook — an avid traveler and lifelong learner who brings fresh perspectives back to his work. A talented skier, EDM enthusiast, and sharp-witted conversationalist, Greg brings creativity and humanity into a field often dominated by numbers. He is respected not only for his expertise but also for his ability to connect with clients and colleagues alike.

Mary Madeline Kelly, Kelly Financial Services

1. **"Do not continue doing what is comfortable.** Pop taught us that in order to be our best selves and grow in life, we must get out of our comfort zone. As much as I hate being uncomfortable, it makes it worth it in the end when you become really good at something."

2. **"Ask a lot of questions.** Even if you were born a genius, you do not know everything. The biggest way to learn about life is to ask questions. You may get the wrong answer at times, but you will figure it out by continuing to ask people questions. Also, take advantage of our access to resources at the tip of our fingers. But at the same time, be weary of the source."

3. **"Show respect to everyone.** No matter who they are or where they come from, respect people. Try not to talk behind people's backs because it will come back to bite you."

4. **"Family is most important.** These are the people who have your best interest in mind no matter what. Tell them you love them often."

5. **"INVEST IN THE STOCK MARKET, ASAP.** The longer you wait the less your money will be compounded over time."

A closer look at Mary Madeline Kelly

Mary Madeline Kelly is a registered financial advisor at Kelly Financial Services, where she has grown up immersed in the family business. She started her humble career secretly eating dinner rolls underneath draped tables at seminars. A graduate of Providence College with a degree in finance, she now works directly with clients on retirement planning and portfolio design while pursuing her goal of becoming an estate-planning attorney.

Mary Madeline is known for her discipline, empathy, and sharp mind. From her early days helping at KFS events as a child to her current role guiding families through complex financial decisions, she has always embodied both professionalism and care. She is also a world traveler, devoted sister, and dog mom whose curiosity and sense of humor light up every room she enters.

Mike Doucette, Kelly Financial Services

1. "**Credit.** Build up your credit. You'll probably purchase an estate [house and surrounding land] at some point. A credit card is important, at a low limit, but it'll help you tremendously when you do it properly and get a good credit score."

2. "**Invest now.** Even if it's $25 a month. Just see how the investment world works, feel the ups and downs. Learn how to make a trade."

3. "**Build up your savings.** It's true for anybody. Have it so you can take advantage of opportunities you see."

4. "**With everything going with crypto, down the road we could end up with digital currency.** I believe it's inevitable, so maybe in addition to savings, save with some crypto too."

5. "**It is never too early to budget at a young age.** Gas, coffee, lunch, clothing, it all adds up. Getting in the habit of a monthly budget is only helpful."

A closer look at Mike Doucette

Michael Doucette is chief operating officer at Kelly Financial Services and a licensed investment advisor representative, bringing more than twenty-five years of experience to the firm. Prior to joining KFS, he held leadership roles at Pioneer Financial Group, The Bulfinch Group, Penn Mutual, and Baystate Financial, where he established a reputation for analytical rigor, client advocacy, and team leadership.

A graduate of Saint Anselm College, Mike combines deep industry expertise with a people-first approach. He has been recognized for both his professional leadership and his mentoring of younger advisors. Away from the office, he is a devoted husband and father of three, active in his community, and known for his dry wit and competitive streak in everything from lawn care to cornhole.

Greg Workman, Kelly Financial Services

1. "**Travel.** See and experience the world throughout your life. Mark Twain famously said, 'Travel is fatal to prejudice, bigotry, and narrow-mindedness.'"

2. "**It's about the journey, <u>not</u> the destination.** Learn to embrace and appreciate the entire process of achievement (the difficult struggles, self-doubt, obstacles, etc.). Actively accept and learn from hardship instead of trying to avoid it. 'I am always doing that which I cannot do, in order that I may learn how to do it.' — Pablo Picasso"

3. "**Continuously learn,** maintain a strong sense of curiosity, and develop new skills throughout your life. Mahatma Gandhi said, 'Live as if you were to die tomorrow; learn as if you were to live forever.'"

4. "**Fear only exists in the mind.** Be bold, take chances and embrace risk — especially at a young age when you can capitalize on and learn from your failures. "Life shrinks or expands in proportion to one's courage.' — Anais Nin"

5. "**Seek out and maintain meaningful relationships** that lift you up and make you the best version of yourself. Research consistently shows that having strong, supportive friendships is significantly linked to living a longer life. 'Friends are the family you choose.' — Jess C. Scott"

A closer look at Greg Workman

Greg Workman is an investment advisor at Kelly Financial Services and holds designations including Accredited Investment Fiduciary® (AIF®), National Social Security Advisor Certificate Holder (NSSA), and Long-Term Care Professional (LTCP). His career in financial services includes roles at Brown Brothers Harriman, Morgan Stanley, New York Life, and Pioneer Financial Group, giving him a breadth of experience across wealth management and insurance.

A graduate of UMass Dartmouth with additional study at Harvard, Greg has a professional foundation rooted in both technical knowledge and communication. He is an accomplished public speaker, a passionate coach, and an active community member. His enthusiasm, curiosity, and commitment to lifelong learning make him a valued advisor and colleague. Most importantly, Greg is a devoted husband and loving father of twins.

Kelly Kelly, Kelly Financial Services

1. "**Invest in yourself and your personal development.** Budget for it. Read *How to Win Friends and Influence People* by Dale Carnegie. I watch a success mentor named Darren Hardy every morning, early with my cup of coffee. Starting the day positively will only return you with positive results."

2. "**Be bold.** Don't be afraid to step out of your comfort zone. One step at a time, and one day at a time. Most importantly — visualize what you want."

3. "**Be you!** It's the best business advice ever received from your father."

4. "**No matter what job you do, be the best at it.** Be on time. The experience is how you position it. In your mind is reality."

5. "**Always have a budget.** Set aside money to invest and compound. Read the *Compound Effect* by Darren Hardy (small book, great read)."

6. "Bonus: Don't let someone tell you that you cannot do something because you are too young, or too old. **Age has no meaning** if you are passionate about something."

A closer look at Kelly Kelly

Kelly Kelly is cofounder, president, and chief executive officer of Kelly Financial Services. Since launching the firm in 2003 with her late husband, Bill Kelly, she has overseen its growth into one of New England's leading independent financial advisory firms. She has served as COO and now CEO, with a focus on both business operations and client experience. She also co-hosts the firm's long-running radio program, *Safe Money Strategies*™.

Kelly is a Georgia native and Valdosta State alum who brings both southern warmth and sharp business acumen to everything she does. To many, she is a role model of resilience and leadership in the financial industry. To her family, she is Mom — steadfast, supportive, and the heart of the Kelly legacy.

Charles Gable, Kelly Financial Services

1. "**Begin investing as early as possible**. Establishing an investment portfolio at a young age leverages the power of compound interest, allowing even modest contributions to grow significantly over time. By starting early, you also gain valuable experience and the flexibility to adjust your strategy as your financial goals evolve."

2. "**Contribute regularly to your investments**. Frequent, consistent contributions — whether weekly, monthly, or quarterly — help smooth out market fluctuations. This practice, often known as dollar-cost averaging, not only instills discipline but also reduces the temptation to time the market."

3. "**Develop a tailored savings plan** and craft a personal budget that aligns with your lifestyle and long-term objectives. This should include specific savings goals (e.g., an emergency fund or a down payment on a home) and designated percentages of your income allocated for each purpose. A structured plan promotes better tracking of progress and fosters healthy financial habits."

4. "**Pay yourself first to prioritize saving** or investing a portion of your income before allocating funds to monthly expenses. By automating transfers into your savings and investment accounts, you remove the guesswork — and potential overspending — while ensuring your future financial well-being remains a top priority."

5. "**Live within your means**, resist the urge to spend money you do not have, and avoid taking on unnecessary debt. Consistently review and adjust your budget to align with your income. Exercising restraint on discretionary purchases and focusing on needs rather than wants will safeguard your financial health and strengthen your long-term security."

A closer look at Charles (Charlie) Gable

Charles "Charlie" Gable is a Financial Advisor at Kelly Financial Services, where he focuses on retirement planning, portfolio design, and client education. His previous experience includes positions at Merrill

Edge, Wells Fargo Advisors, Webster Investments, and Commonwealth Financial Group.

A graduate of Babson College, Charlie combines technical expertise with a practical, approachable style. He is also an active athlete and volunteer, bringing the same energy to his community that he brings to his client work. Charlie's clients and colleagues know him as dedicated, disciplined, and always willing to go the extra mile. Charlie's primary focus in life is his family, being an excellent father and husband.

CHAPTER 16

Final Remarks

My Parting Advice

Τhis book was a project on a whim. It started with a quark. Most of all, I knew it needed to be done, because there is such a lack of financial education in, well, the education system (among other reasons). I, from the deepest part of my heart, hope it helps you. I want to wrap up this book with some parting words, more personal rather than financial education.

Doubters in life? Ignore Them!
Anytime you or someone you know tells you that you can't do something, **ignore them!**

I've had many doubters in my life, and unfortunately, I believed them before. But as I got older, I learned:

- People's words act as mirrors, reflecting how they see the world rather than how it truly is.
- They are very unqualified to make that judgment.
- In hindsight, I shouldn't have taken them seriously.

How many people have experienced tragedy, heartbreak, bullies, fear, doubt, or shortcomings, and let it stop them, even if it's an irrational decision to do so?

How many others overcame those same challenges and decided to make it happen anyway?

Both crowds contain a large number of people, so at the end of the day, who would you like to be? I bet I know the answer. First and foremost, don't let anyone throw you off course or diminish your self-worth, esteem, intelligence, or abilities. Don't let them past your "mental barrier." Especially don't allow them to become obstacles when it comes to taking your personal finances and future seriously at a young age. Don't let "some schmuck make you spend money on a friend group vacation if you aren't ready," type of thing.

What someone says doesn't make it reality. You will experience failure in life; without it, you wouldn't be able to succeed. Focus on your own growing pains and refuse to let others get in the way of what you do. Simple as that. If you're in search of deeper advice, go to the previous chapter.

My Personal Journey and Why I Never Gave Up

I lost my father when I was very young, eleven years old to be exact. I am blessed to have such an amazing and strong family, but even with one, not having your key male figure in your life is statistically harmful to young men's futures. However, I found my way and became my own man. It took a lot of work, mistakes, and trials along the way. However, I never realized how atypical my journey was until I spoke with our family friend, and whom I refer to as my "honorary" uncle, Jeff Kuhner, after our phone interview for "Voices of the Masters." He said:

> "Most kids from your situation never make it. You graduated from one of the most difficult high schools in North America. You're pursuing a career in one of the most noble professions. You're writing this book. I know your father is beaming down from heaven."

I never thought about it. I was just focused on my projects, but Jeff was right. It made me see what I'd really accomplished despite the adversity I faced during my childhood. Just as a couple examples:

- **I created my own company at nineteen**, something I only thought people in their thirties did. Personally, for me, I wanted to do it earlier than later.
- **After becoming an entrepreneur**, I wrote and published this book (with the guidance of some amazing people) to help young Americans navigate their financial future. I NEVER GAVE UP!

- **I became a wrestler** with no qualifications whatsoever. However, I had a coach who instilled lifelong values and never gave up on me. Sometimes, we focus on not quitting ourselves but having someone who always believes in you can be a blessing. I graduated having received the U.S. Marine Corps and Wrestling Coaches Association Leadership and Character Award and became a New England qualifier (plus most improved!). Wrestling, especially, taught me not to quit. If you've wrestled, you understand.

- **I became a powerlifter and** hold multiple state records. I have a deep appreciation for this sport, and the fact it pushes the limits of the human body. In my opinion, wrestling and powerlifting go hand-in-hand.

Bill Kelly's Lesson to Me

My father always taught me there is no greater service you can provide in life than to help people. When I say I hope I have helped you, I mean I hope I transformed your financial future in the most positive respect and permanent way, even if all I provided was financial education and interviews.

So, on that note, to help kickstart some of your financial goals, let me slide you a few things I've learned:

1. **Watch the news and think critically.** Small or specialized news sources you can read often provide more detailed insight, but make sure you're using your own judgment. This helps you gauge investment opportunities when major events happen. For instance, if 50 percent of the peanut industry got wiped out by a hurricane, that's a potential regrowth opportunity for the long term after it is rehabilitated.

2. **Read, read, and did I mention read?** Immerse yourself in financial literature, or any topic that opens your mind. Don't stress about devouring it all at once. Make it a daily habit if you're new, fifteen pages a day can be enough to start. Let the words come to you. A few books I enjoyed:

   - *Common Sense on Mutual Funds: New Imperatives for the Intelligent Investor* by John C. Bogle

- *Capitalism and Freedom* by Milton Friedman
- *Small Giants* by Bo Burlingham
- *Zconomy* by Jason R. Dorsey and Denise Villa, PhD
- *One Up on Wall Street* by Peter Lynch with John Rothchild

These aren't all strictly on the same topic, but they helped expand my sphere of thinking. Browse Thrift Books (great for second-hand cheap finds), Barnes & Noble, or wherever. Just dive into new ideas!

3. **Research media, books, and people.** Gauge perspectives and reviews. Sometimes you learn crucial info from observing how other people see a product, service, or idea. Bill Ackman is a pro at this.

4. **Prioritize education.** Kelly Financial Services emphasize this with their clients, and it applies to you, also. The more you understand, the more confident you become, and as an added bonus, you become a better investor.

Thank you for letting me be part of your journey. It's an opportunity at your fingertips: time, investment possibilities, and the knowledge you've gained. Remember, investing involves risk, including potentially losing your principal. Markets are volatile, and there are no guarantees of profit or protection against loss. However, this is where education, financial professionals, and (like we've previously discussed) diligence come in to mitigate those inherent risks.

Wherever you go and whatever you do, remember you have the power to change your financial future. Do not forget the potential you have, especially if you're part of my generation, because you have time on your side. If there's one phrase I hope echoes in your mind, it's **never give up**. I look forward to writing another book, maybe covering more complicated topics, strategies, and education.

If you have questions, want to share your progress, or have feedback, reach out to me: **williamkellyjr@kellyfinancial.org**. If the book helps, or impacts you, **please tell me how.** If you have criticism or questions, send them my way as well. *Please note that I am not a financial adviser, and any correspondence is for general discussion or educational purposes only — I cannot provide any individualized investment or financial advice.*

It's an honor to be part of your story, and I look forward to hearing from you. Now, get after your great financial future!

Thank you for reading. Be well.

William Kelly
Author

This material is provided for educational purposes only and does not constitute investment, legal, or tax advice. Investing involves risk, including possible loss of principal. Kelly Financial Services is a Registered Investment Adviser. Registration does not imply a certain level of skill or training.

CHAPTER 17

Chapter Navigation

Introduction
Why this book, why now? William makes the case that Gen Z can turn work into lasting wealth with the right guidance and habits, and he invites you to let him help you start. Keywords: purpose, Gen Z, mindset, guidance, habits.

What Are the Chances?
How to think like an investor: evaluate businesses based on fundamentals and values, maintain discipline during volatility and learn quickly from sunk costs rather than clinging to them. **Keywords**: discipline, fundamentals, values, sunk cost, patience.

Budgets, Buffers, and Big Flex Credit
Track your cash, sort fixed vs. variable costs, and build an emergency fund so surprises don't wreck your vibe. Use credit wisely to boost your score. As income grows, increase investing (around 15% pre-tax). Organize the bag, pad the buffer, flex responsibly. **Keywords**: budgeting, emergency fund, credit score, investing, financial independence.

Never Forget the Dutch
A quick history of public markets — from the Dutch East India Company to today — introduces the four core public assets (stocks, bonds, ETFs, mutual funds) that form the foundation for building wealth. **Keywords**: history, markets, stocks, bonds, ETFs.

Speculation vs. Investing

William draws a clear line: investing means owning value for the long term, while speculation is betting on short-term price moves. Discover the patient playbook (Buffett, Bogle, Lynch) and learn when — even sparingly — speculation can have its place. **Keywords**: long term, patience, fundamentals, hype, timing.

Curiosity Killed the Investor

A Q&A grab-bag of real reader questions on habits, accounts, school vs. debt, and "What should I actually do now?" — featuring practical guidance that emphasizes consistent investing and informed decision-making. **Keywords**: FAQs, habits, college, debt, action steps.

The Dynamic Duo, Squared

Retirement freedom isn't abstract — William explains how pairing tax-deferred with tax-free accounts (and layering employer plans) creates compounding "duos" that stack toward the life you want. **Keywords**: retirement, tax-deferred, tax-free, strategy, planning.

No Falling in the Pit

Two cautionary tales (Emily vs. John; Sam's debt spiral) highlight the importance of early, consistent investing and the dangers of lifestyle debt — helping you steer clear of penalties, hype chasing, and years of credit repair. **Keywords**: pitfalls, debt, compounding, behavior, discipline.

What-a Portafoglio!

Define the toolkit: portfolios, equities, diversification, risk tolerance, volatility, capital gains, and asset allocation — so you can craft a lineup that matches your goals (not someone else's template). **Keywords**: portfolio, diversification, risk, allocation, terms.

Whatcha See Is Whatcha Get

Taxes are everywhere. This chapter demystifies federal, state, and local taxes while highlighting tax-efficient vehicles (e.g., HSAs, 529s) to help more of your money compound for you. **Keywords**: taxes, efficiency, HSAs, 529s, planning.

Compound Effect

The engine of wealth: earnings that earn on themselves. Start early, automate your contributions, and let time do the heavy lifting. **Keywords**: compounding, automation, time, contributions.

Time Has Come Today

A debt playbook: what's "good" (mortgages) vs. "bad" (credit cards, and often student loans), balance transfers, side-income, and avalanche vs. snowball payoff strategies — helping you exit debt and get back to growth. **Keywords**: debt, avalanche, snowball, mortgages, strategy.

Show Me the Way

Turn knowledge into action: choose a brokerage, invest in what you understand, diversify, and select from sample allocations (ranging from very aggressive to very conservative) aligned with your risk tolerance. **Keywords**: brokerage, allocation, diversification, models, execution.

Crypto

Approach crypto as a fast-evolving frontier: educate yourself first, start with small, manageable amounts, and prioritize risk management. Only invest what you can afford to lose — curiosity encouraged, but avoid getting swept up in the hype. **Keywords**: crypto, risk, learning, volatility, frontier.

Voices of the Masters

A curated chorus of five-point playbooks from diverse pros — covering living within your means, starting early, building credit, investing wisely, and staying resilient — so you can borrow their best habits. **Keywords**: mentors, advice, habits, careers, resilience.

Voices of Kelly Financial Services

From one firm, a unified team shares hard-earned wisdom — strategic planning, the role of family, courage, and disciplined savings — to guide your next move. **Keywords**: travel, relationships, bold, savings, education.

Final Remarks

A closing charge to keep learning, keep contributing, and keep your plan simple and consistent — because the compounding future you desire is shaped by what you do next. **Keywords**: call to action, consistency, learning, next steps.

Acknowledgments

I give a special thanks to the many people who helped me write this book with your knowledge and spirit.

Kelly Kelly, Mary Madeline Kelly, Walter "Poppy" Schroer, "Pyroman" John Budris, "British Voiceover" Rob Townsend, Mike Meek, Mike "Bulldog" McClarney, Dr. Grace Vuoto and Jeffery Kuhner, Mark O'ffill, Lloyd Granoff, Jamie Serrano, David Callanan, Bob and Rose Grace, Kevin Haskin, Carey Kennedy, Ryan Schlesener, and my friends.

And of course, thanks to our entire team at **Kelly Financial**, along with **many, many more.**

Honorable mentions: my assistants (cat and dog) Marshall and Georgia.

About the Author

WILLIAM KELLY

William Kelly is one of America's youngest voices in financial education, a portfolio entrepreneur, and fintech start-up founder dedicated to making investing more accessible to the next generation. He is also a co-host of the popular Boston radio programs *Safe Money Strategies* on WRKO 680 AM and *Saturday Night Safe Money Strategies* on WBZ 1030 AM, where he blends practical guidance with clear, relatable storytelling.

Born into a family business deeply rooted in financial planning, William grew up learning the principles of long-term wealth building from some of the industry's top professionals. By the time he was a teenager, he had already spent countless hours in client meetings, sharpening the skills and perspective that fuel his mission today: empowering young people to invest early and wisely.

A frequent traveler to Switzerland, England, Italy, Spain, and Canada, William draws inspiration from global markets and cultures. His experiences abroad, combined with nearly two years living in the Dominican Republic, shaped his passion for financial literacy as a tool for independence and opportunity.

Beyond finance, William is a powerlifter, youth coach, student, speaker, traveler, radio contributor, article contributor, philanthropist, advocate for libertarianism, and free market principles.

Only the Good Invest Young is his debut book, written to equip his peers with the confidence, strategies, and mindset to take control of their financial journeys.

www.ingramcontent.com/pod-product-compliance
Lightning Source LLC
Chambersburg PA
CBHW071849200326
41519CB00016B/4297